ENGLISH SCOTTISH AND WELSH
LANDSCAPE

ENGLISH SCOTTISH AND WELSH LANDSCAPE

1700–*c.* 1860

CHOSEN BY JOHN BETJEMAN
AND GEOFFREY TAYLOR

WITH

ORIGINAL LITHOGRAPHS

By

JOHN PIPER

GRANGER POETRY LIBRARY

GRANGER BOOK CO., INC.
Great Neck, N.Y.

First Published 1944
Reprinted 1978

International Standard Book Number 0-89609-080-9

Library of Congress Catalog Number 77-094807

PRINTED IN THE UNITED STATES OF AMERICA

APOLOGY

WELL may the critical exclaim, Where are Spenser, Keats and Hardy? Why so much Tennyson? Who are all these unknown clergymen? To explain the seeming disproportion will be to describe the scope of this book.

We were given three thousand lines for a *representative* anthology of landscape poetry. We confined ourselves to the most prolific period, 1700 to about 1860, and to non-copyright poems. We chose inland scenery and concentrated on country subjects. We demanded that the poet should have obviously looked at and loved what he described.

You must visualize the earlier part of the book at any rate, as a series of views of this island rendered by oil, water-colour or engraving. Cunningham's conventional landscapes have been well described by Mr. Grigson in *The Romantics* as 'like a vast oil on a dining-room wall in an eighteenth-century mansion—the kind that goes with the house because it is too big for the auctioneer to sell'. The wooden passage from Dodsley is like an inn signboard: Bampfylde is a Morland: Goldsmith is some not very good picture, but so famous that it could not be omitted: Crabbe has the freshness of a Cotman water-colour: many of the lesser-known writers round the turn of the century are like the copper engravings or Bewick cuts which, no doubt, adorned some of their works. But thereafter the parallel between artist and poet becomes more debatable. The best most pre-Raphaelites could do for Tennyson was to paint his legendary figures.

With this pictorial object before us, we made big decisions about some major poets within the period. However beautiful, no historical nor tapestry scenes could be admitted. Keats, Hood, Darley and Shelley wrote landscape poetry, rarely of a particular scene or season, and either forming part of a poem which would suffer greatly by cutting or presenting an example of landscape verse no better and often worse than less-appreciated contemporaries. From Wordsworth, the greatest poet of the period, we could have made a volume this length of pure description. But Wordsworth would have suffered. He unrolls slowly in great strips—description, meditation, worship—and the passages we include give as much

v

of Wordsworth's moods before landscape as space allows. But Tennyson, that great sardonic Lincolnshire humorist, is easily quotable. Space caused us reluctantly to exclude passages from Browning's *Inn Album*, Byron's *Newstead Abbey* and the ten final stanzas of the *Scholar Gipsy;* the last are not descriptive. Four or five passages from every other poet included had to be cut, and many excellent poets like Sotheby and Kennish were omitted from the less-known.

As for these lesser-known people—quiet Georgian rectors, village schoolmasters, peers in their libraries looking across the park, Victorian drunks and reformers and escapists—they are the reason for the book. They were recording landscape from the distant view to the cascade in a wet cart rut, with a love and observation men are just beginning again to appreciate. Theirs may be 'pedestrian' verse, but it is written by pedestrians or, at the fastest, travellers on a cob, for pedestrians. Heaven knows how many of these faithful poets have disappeared in the paper salvage campaign nor how many survive on the sixpenny shelves in old book shops. In Allibone's Dictionary (by no means complete) the following tempting poets whom we have been unable to obtain appear under part of letter B alone:

Henry Baker (Essays, Pastoral and Elegiac), 1756; Thomas Baker (Winter), 1767; — Bakewell (The Moorland Bard), 1807; Henry Barwick (Nature, a Poem), 1807; Edward Beavan (Box Hill), 1777; Mrs. Bowen (Ystradffin, a Descriptive Poem); Robert Bradstreet (The Sabine Farm), 1818; Moses Brown (Percy Lodge), 1755; Anne Bryton (Richmond), 1780.

To these and all other such poets in the alphabet we extend our hearty good wishes and sincere hopes for a speedy revival in a larger anthology than this.

We wish to express our indebtedness for help and encouragement to Messrs. Edmund Blunden, Eric Partridge, Lady Chetwode, M. J. Craig, J. Arlott, J. N. Bryson, A. H. R. Elton, and our gratitude to Mr. John Piper for his sympathetic illustrations which are largely deliberately unconnected with individual poems.

J. B.

Easter Day 1943.   G. T.

Pistyll Cain   *North Wales*

ANNE, COUNTESS OF WINCHELSEA 1661-1720

A NOCTURNAL REVERIE
Wiltshire

In such a night when every louder wind
Is to its distant cavern safe confin'd;
And only gentle Zephyr fans its wings,
And lonely Philomel, still waking, sings;
Or from some tree, fam'd for the owl's delight,
She, hollowing clear, directs the wand'rer right;
In such a night, when passing clouds give place,
Or thinly veil the heaven's mysterious face;
When in some river overhung with green,
The waving moon and trembling leaves are seen;
When fresh'ned grass now bears itself upright,
And makes cool banks to pleasing rest invite,
Whence springs the woodbine and the bramble-rose,
And where the sleepy cowslip shelter'd grows;
Whilst now a paler hue the foxglove takes,
Yet chequers still with red the dusky brakes,
When scatter'd glow-worms, but in twilight fine,
Show trivial beauties watch their hour to shine;
While Salisbury stands the test of every light,
In perfect charm and perfect virtue bright;
When odours, which declin'd repelling day,
Thro' temp'rate air uninterrupted stray;
When darken'd groves their softest shadows wear,
And falling waters we distinctly hear;
When thro' the gloom more venerable shows
Some ancient fabric, awful in repose,
While sunburnt hills their swarthy looks conceal,
And swelling haycocks thicken up the vale;
When the loos'd horse now, as his pasture leads,
Comes slowly grazing thro' th'adjoining meads
Whose stealing pace, and lengthen'd shade we fear,
Till torn-up forage in his teeth we hear:
When nibbling sheep at large pursue their food,
And unmolested kine rechew the cud;

I

When curlews cry beneath the village walls,
And to her straggling brood the partridge calls;
Their short-lived jubilee the creatures keep,
Which but endures whilst tyrant man does sleep;
When a sedate content the spirit feels,
And no fierce light disturbs, whilst it reveals,
But silent musings urge the mind to seek
Something too high for syllables to speak;
Till the free soul to a compos'dness charm'd,
Finding the elements of rage disarm'd,
O'er all below, a solemn quiet grown,
Joys in th' inferior world and thinks it like her own:
In such a night let me abroad remain,
Till morning breaks, and all's confus'd again:
Our cares, our toils, our clamours are renew'd,
Or pleasures, seldom reach'd, again pursued.

JOHN GAY 1685–1732

from

AN EPISTLE TO THE RIGHT HONOURABLE
THE EARL OF BURLINGTON

Here sheep the pasture hide, there harvests bend,
See Sarum's steeple o'er yon hill ascend;
Our horses faintly trot beneath the heat,
And our keen stomachs know the hour to eat.
Who can forsake thy walls, and not admire
The proud Cathedral, and the lofty spire?
What sempstress has not prov'd thy scissors good?
From hence first came th' intriguing riding-hood.
Amid three boarding-schools well stock'd with misses,
Shall three knights-errant starve for want of kisses?

O'er the green turf the miles slide swift away,
And Blandford ends the labours of the day.
The morning rose; the supper reck'ning paid,
And our due fees discharg'd to man and maid,
The ready ostler near the stirrup stands,
And as we mount, our half-pence load his hands.

Now the steep hill fair Dorchester o'erlooks,
Border'd by meads, and wash'd by silver brooks . . .
Now o'er true Roman way our horses sound,
Graevius would kneel, and kiss the sacred ground.
On either side low fertile valleys lie,
The distant prospects tire the trav'ling eye.
Through Bridport's stony lanes our route we take,
And the proud steep descend to Morcombe's lake.
As hearses pass'd, our landlord robb'd the pall,
And with the mournful scutcheon hung his hall.
On unadulterate wine we here regale,
And strip the lobster of his scarlet mail.
  We climb'd the hills when starry night arose,
And Axminster affords a kind repose.
The maid subdued by fees, her trunk unlocks,
And gives the cleanly aid of dowlas smocks.
Meantime our shirts her busy fingers rub,
While the soap lathers o'er the foaming tub.
If women's gear such pleasing dreams incite,
Lend us your smocks, ye damsels, ev'ry night! . . .
  Now from the steep, midst scatter'd cotts and groves,
Our eye through Honiton's fair valley roves.
Behind us soon the busy town we leave,
Where finest lace industrious lasses weave.
Now swelling clouds roll'd on; the rainy load
Stream'd down our hats, and smoked along the road;
When (O blest sight!) a friendly sign we spied,
Our spurs are slacken'd from the horse's side;
For sure a civil host the house commands,
Upon whose sign this courteous motto stands.
This is the ancient hand, and eke the pen;
Here is for horses hay, and meat for men.

from

TO A LADY BEFORE MARRIAGE

In some small hamlet on the lonely plain,
Where Thames, thro' meadows, rolls his mazy train;
Or where high Windsor, thick with greens array'd,
Waves his old oaks, and spreads his ample shade,
Fancy has figur'd out our calm retreat;
Already round the visionary seat
Our limes begin to shoot, our flow'rs to spring,
The brooks to murmur, and the birds to sing.
Where dost thou lie, thou thinly-peopled green?
Thou nameless lawn, and village yet unseen?
Where sons, contented with their native ground,
Ne'er travell'd further than ten furlongs round;
And the tann'd peasant, and his ruddy bride,
Were born together, and together died.
Where early larks best tell the morning-light,
And only Philomel disturbs the night,
'Midst gardens here my humble pile shall rise,
With sweets surrounded of ten thousand dyes;
All savage where th'embroider'd gardens end,
The haunt of echoes shall my woods ascend;
And O! if heav'n th'ambitious thought approve,
A rill shall warble cross the gloomy grove,
A little rill, o'er pebbly beds convey'd,
Gush down the steep, and glitter thro' the glade.
What cheering scents those bord'ring banks exhale!
How loud that heifer lows from yonder vale!
That thrush, how shrill! his note so clear, so high,
He drowns each feather'd minstrel of the sky.
Here let me trace, beneath the purpled morn,
The deep-mouth'd beagle, and the sprightly horn;
Or lure the trout with well-dissembled flies,
Or fetch the flutt'ring partridge from the skies;
Nor shall thy hand disdain to crop the vine,
The downy peach, or flavour'd nectarine;
Or rob the bee-hive of its golden hoard,
And bear th'unbought luxuriance to thy board.

4

Weathercote Cave *Yorkshire*

ALEXANDER POPE 1688-1744

from

WINDSOR FOREST

Berkshire

With slaught'ring guns th' unwearied fowler roves,
When frosts have whiten'd all the naked groves;
Where doves in flocks the leafless trees o'ershade,
And lonely woodcocks haunt the wat'ry glade.
He lifts the tube, and levels with his eye;
Straight a short thunder breaks the frozen sky:
Oft, as in airy rings they skim the heath,
The clam'rous lapwings feel the leaden death:
Oft, as the mounting larks their notes prepare,
They fall, and leave their little lives in air.

REV. ROBERT BLAIR 1699-1746

from

THE GRAVE

East Lothian

See yonder hallow'd fane! the pious work
Of names once famed, now dubious or forgot,
And buried 'midst the wreck of things which were;
There lie interr'd the more illustrious dead.
The wind is up: hark! how it howls! methinks,
Till now I never heard a sound so dreary.
Doors creak, and windows clap, and night's foul bird,
Rook'd in the spire, screams loud, the gloomy aisles,
Black plaster'd, and hung round with shreds of scutcheons
And tatter'd coats of arms, send back the sound,
Laden with heavier airs, from the low vaults,
The mansions of the dead! Roused from their slumbers,
In grim array the grisley spectres rise,
Grin horrible, and obstinately sullen
Pass and repass, hush'd as the foot of night!
Again the screech owl shrieks; ungracious sound!
I'll hear no more; it makes one's blood run chill.

5

Quite round the pile, a row of reverend elms,
Coeval near with that, all ragged show,
Long lash'd by the rude winds; some rift half down
Their branchless trunks, others so thin a-top
That scarce two crows could lodge in the same tree . . .
    Oft in the lone church-yard at night I've seen,
By glimpse of moon-shine, chequering through the trees,
The school-boy, with his satchel in his hand,
Whistling aloud to bear his courage up,
And lightly tripping o'er the long flat stones
(With nettles skirted and with moss o'ergrown)
That tell in homely phrase who lie below.
Sudden he starts! and hears, or thinks he hears,
The sound of something purring at his heels.
Full fast he flies, and dares not look behind him,
Till out of breath he overtakes his fellows,
Who gather round and wonder at the tale.

REV. JOHN DYER 1700–1758

from

GRONGAR HILL

Carmarthen

Wide and wider spreads the vale,
As circles on a smooth canal:
The mountains round, unhappy fate!
Sooner or later, of all height,
Withdraw their summits from the skies,
And lessen as the others rise:
Still the prospect wider spreads,
Adds a thousand woods and meads,
Still it widens, widens still,
And sinks the newly-risen hill.
    Now I gain the mountain's brow,
What a landscape lies below!
No clouds, no vapours intervene,
But the gay, the open scene
Does the face of Nature show,
In all the hues of Heaven's bow!

And, swelling to embrace the light,
Spreads around beneath the sight.
   Old castles on the cliffs arise,
Proudly towering in the skies!
Rushing from the woods, the spires
Seem from hence ascending fires!
Half his beams Apollo sheds
On the yellow mountain-heads!
Gilds the fleeces of the flocks:
And glitters on the broken rocks!
   Below me trees unnumbered rise,
Beautiful in various dyes:
The gloomy pine, the poplar blue,
The yellow beech, the sable yew,
The slender fir that taper grows,
The sturdy oak with broad-spread boughs.
And beyond, the purple grove,
Haunt of Phillis queen of love!
Gaudy as the opening dawn,
Lies a long and level lawn,
On which a dark hill, steep and high,
Holds and charms the wandering eye!
Deep are his feet in Towy's flood,
His sides are cloth'd with waving wood,
And ancient towers crown his brow,
That cast an awful look below;
Whose ragged walls the ivy creeps,
And with her arms from falling keeps;
So both a safety from the wind
On mutual dependence find.
   'Tis now the raven's bleak abode;
'Tis now th' apartment of the toad;
And there the fox securely feeds;
And there the poisonous adder breeds,
Concealed in ruins, moss and weeds,
While, ever and anon, there falls
Huge heaps of hoary mouldered walls.
Yet time has seen, that lifts the low,
And level lays the lofty brow,
Has seen this broken pile complete,

7

Big with the vanity of state;
But transient is the smile of fate! . . .
    Ever charming, ever new,
When will the landscape tire the view!
The fountain's fall, the river's flow,
The woody valleys, warm and low;
The windy summit, wild and high,
Roughly rushing on the sky!
The pleasant seat, the ruined tower,
The naked rock, the shady bower;
The town and village, dome and farm,
Each give each a double charm,
As pearls upon an Æthiop's arm.

    See on the mountain's southern side,
Where the prospect opens wide,
Where the evening gilds the tide;
How close and small the hedges lie!
What streaks of meadows cross the eye!
A step methinks may pass the stream,
So little distant dangers seem;
So we mistake the future's face,
Eyed through hope's deluding glass;
As yon summits soft and fair,
Clad in colours of the air,
Which to those who journey near,
Barren, brown, and rough appear;
Still we tread the same coarse way,
The present's still a cloudy day.

JAMES THOMSON 1700–1748

THE SEASONS

SPRING

As yet the trembling year is unconfirmed,
And Winter oft at eve resumes the breeze,
Chills the pale morn, and bids his driving sleets
Deform the day delightless; so that scarce
The bittern knows his time, with bill engulfed,
To shake the sounding marsh; or, from the shore,

The plovers when to scatter o'er the heath,
And sing their wild notes to the listening waste.

At last from Aries rolls the bounteous sun,
And the bright Bull receives him. Then no more
The expansive atmosphere is cramped with cold;
But, full of life and vivifying soul,
Lifts the light clouds sublime, and spreads them thin,
Fleecy, and white, o'er all-surrounding heaven.

Forth fly the tepid airs; and, unconfined,
Unbinding earth, the moving softness strays.
Joyous, the impatient husbandman perceives
Relenting nature, and his lusty steers
Drives from their stalls to where the well-used plough
Lies in the furrow, loosened from the frost.
There, unrefusing, to the harnessed yoke
They lend their shoulder, and begin their toil,
Cheered by the simple song and soaring lark.
Meanwhile incumbent o'er the shining share
The master leans, removes the obstructing clay,
Winds the whole work, and sidelong lays the glebe.

White, through the neighbouring fields, the sower stalks
With measured step; and, liberal, throws the grain
Into the faithful bosom of the ground.
The harrow follows harsh, and shuts the scene.

from

THE SEASONS

AUTUMN

But see the fading many-coloured woods,
Shade deepening over shade, the country round
Imbrown; a crowded umbrage, dusk and dun,
Of every hue, from wan declining green
To sooty dark. These now the lonesome muse,
Low-whispering, lead into their leaf-strown walks,
And give the season in its latest view.

Meantime, light shadowing all, a sober calm
Fleeces unbounded ether; whose least wave
Stands tremulous, uncertain where to turn
The gentle current; while, illumined wide,
The dewy-skirted clouds imbibe the sun,
And through their lucid veil his softened force
Shed o'er the peaceful world. Then is the time
For those whom widsom and whom nature charm
To steal themselves from the degenerate crowd,
And soar above this little scene of things;
To tread low-thoughted vice beneath their feet,
To soothe the throbbing passions into peace,
And woo lone quiet in her silent walks.

Thus solitary, and in pensive guise,
Oft let me wander o'er the russet mead,
And through the saddened grove, where scarce is heard
One dying strain to cheer the woodman's toil.
Haply some widowed songster pours his plaint,
Far, in faint warblings, through the tawny copse;
While congregated thrushes, linnets, larks,
And each wild throat, whose artless strains so late
Swelled all the music of the swarming shades,
Robbed of their tuneful souls, now shivering sit
On the dead tree, a dull despondent flock;
With not a brightness waving o'er their plumes,
And naught save chattering discord in their note.
Oh! let not, aimed from some inhuman eye,
The gun the music of the coming year
Destroy; and harmless, unsuspecting harm,
Lay the weak tribes, a miserable prey,
In mingled murder, fluttering on the ground.

Tomen-y-Mur and Roman Amphitheatre

North Wales

from

AGRICULTURE: A POEM
Middlesex

See where the farmer, with a master's eye,
Surveys his little kingdom, and exults
In sov'reign independence. At a word,
His feathery subjects in obedience flock
Around his feeding hand, who in return
Yield a delicious tribute to his board,
And o'er his couch their downy plumage spread.
The peacock here expands his eyeful plumes,
A glittering pageant to the mid-day sun:
In the stiff awkwardness of foolish pride,
The swelling turkey apes his stately step,
And calls the bristling feathers round his head.
There the loud herald of the morning struts
Before his cackling dames, the passive slaves
Of his promiscuous pleasure.   O'er the pond,
See the gray gander, with his female train,
Bending their lofty necks; and gabbling ducks,
Rejoicing on the surface clap their wings;
Whilst wheeling round, in airy wanton flights,
The glossy pigeons chase their sportive loves,
Or in soft cooings tell their amorous tale.
Here stacks of hay, there pyramids of corn,
Promise the future market large supplies:
While with an eye of triumph he surveys
His piles of wood, and laughs at winter's frown.
In silent rumination, see the kine,
Beneath the walnut's shade, patiently wait
To pour into his pails their milky stores.
While pent from mischief, far from sight remov'd,
The bristly herd, within their fatt'ning styes,
Remind him to prepare, in many a row,
The gaily blooming pea, the fragrant bean,
And broad-leav'd cabbage for the ploughman's feast.

11

B

from

THE NOCTURNAL ECLOGUE
Buckinghamshire

Hark! the shrill Cock, the rising Morn proclaims,
And calls aloud to Field his feathery Dames:
The mounting Lark begins her warbling Song,
And general Notes employ the airy Throng.
And, see! the Sun reveals a glimm'ring Ray,
And streaks the bright'ning Clouds with Gleams of Day,
All Nature seems reviving at his Sight,
And, smiling, wakes to hail his amber Light.
Now sparkling Dew-drops glister on the Grain,
And cooly Breezes fan the healthsome Plain;
The Plow-boy, o'er the Furrows, whistles blithe,
And in the Mead the Mower whets his Scythe;
Shrill Horns alarm the Sportsman from his Dream,
And the Bells tinkle on the new-yok'd Team.

REV. STEPHEN DUCK 1705–1756

from

THE THRESHER'S LABOUR
Wiltshire

The Grass again is spread upon the Ground,
Till not a vacant Place is to be found;
And while the parching Sun-beams on it shine,
The Hay-makers have Time allow'd to dine.
That soon dispatch'd, they still sit on the Ground;
And the brisk Chat, renew'd, afresh goes round.
All talk at once; but seeming all to fear,
That what they speak, the rest will hardly hear;
Till by degrees so high their Notes they strain,
A Stander-by can nought distinguish plain.
So loud's their Speech, and so confus'd their Noise,
Scarce puzzled Echo can return the Voice.

Yet, spite of this, they bravely all go on;
Each scorns to be, or seem to be, outdone.
Mean-while the changing Sky begins to lour,
And hollow Winds proclaim a sudden Show'r;
The tattling Croud can scarce their Garments gain,
Before descends the thick impetuous Rain;
Their noisy Prattle all at once is done,
And to the Hedge they soon for Shelter run.

REV. WILLIAM THOMPSON 1712–1766

from

ON LAUREL HILL

Oxfordshire

O Pope! the sweetest of the tuneful race,
This votive tablet, grateful, here I place;
Here, where the Graces sport on Laurel Hill,
Fast by the music of the murmuring rill;
From hence the bluish Berkshire hills survey,
Which oft have echoed to thy sylvan lay;
When young, in Windsor's blissful fields you stray'd,
Immortal by your deathless labours made!
There the first music trembled from thy tongue,
And Binfield swains on every accent hung:
The larks the sweetness of thy notes confest,
And, dumb with envy, sunk into their nest;
While in soft silence Lodden stole along,
And, listening, wonder'd at thy softer song.
Nor scorn the prospects which Oxonia yields,
Her hills as verdant, and as fair her fields.

from

THE INVITATION TO SELBORNE
Hampshire

Oft on some evening, sunny, soft, and still,
The Muse shall lead thee to the beech-grown hill,
To spend in tea the cool, refreshing hour,
Where nods in air the pensile, nest-like bower . . .
Romantic spot! from whence in prospect lies
Whate'er of landscape charms our feasting eyes,
The pointed spire, the hall, the pasture-plain,
The russet fallow, or the golden grain,
The breezy lake that sheds a gleaming light,
Till all the fading picture fail the sight.
    Each to his task; all different ways retire:
Cull the dry stick; call forth the seeds of fire;
Deep fix the kettle's props, a forky row,
Or give with fanning hat the breeze to blow.
    Whence is this taste, the furnish'd hall forgot,
To feast in gardens, or th' unhandy grot?
Or novelty with some new charms surprises,
Or from our very shifts some joy arises.
Hark, while below the village bells ring round,
Echo, sweet nymph, returns the soften'd sound;
But if gusts rise, the rushing forests roar,
Like the tide tumbling on the pebbly shore.

WILLIAM COLLINS 1721–1759

ODE TO EVENING

If ought of Oaten Stop, or Pastoral Song,
May hope, O pensive Eve, to soothe thine Ear,
   Like thy own solemn Springs,
   Thy Springs, and dying Gales,
O Nymph reserv'd, while now the bright-hair'd Sun
Sits in yon western Tent, whose cloudy Skirts,
   With Brede ethereal wove,
   O'erhang his wavy Bed:

Now Air is hush'd, save where the weak-ey'd Bat,
With short shrill Shriek flits by on leathern Wing,
    Or where the Beetle winds
    His small but sullen Horn,
As oft he rises 'midst the twilight Path,
Against the Pilgrim born in heedless Hum:
    Now teach me, Maid compos'd,
    To breathe some soften'd Strain,

Whose Numbers stealing thro' thy dark'ning Vale,
May not unseemly with its Stillness suit,
    As musing slow, I hail
    Thy genial lov'd Return!
For when thy folding Star arising shews
His paly Circlet, at his warning Lamp
    The fragrant Hours, and Elves
    Who slept in Flow'rs the Day,
And many a Nymph who wreathes her Brows with Sedge
And sheds the fresh'ning Dew, and lovelier still,
    The Pensive Pleasures sweet
    Prepare thy shadowy Car.

Then let me rove some wild and heathy scene,
Or find some Ruin, 'midst its dreary dells
    Whose walls more awful nod
    By thy religious Gleams.
Or if chill blust'ring Winds, or driving Rain,
Prevent my willing Feet, be mine the Hut,
    That from the Mountain's Side,
    Views Wilds, and swelling Floods,
And Hamlets brown, and dim-discover'd Spires,
And hears their simple Bell, and marks o'er all
    Thy Dewy Fingers draw
    The gradual dusky Veil.

While Spring shall pour his Show'rs, as oft he wont,
And bathe thy breathing Tresses, meekest Eve!
    While Summer loves to sport,
    Beneath thy ling'ring Light:

While sallow Autumn fills thy Lap with Leaves,
Or Winter yelling thro' the troublous Air,
  Affrights thy shrinking Train,
  And rudely rends thy Robes,
So long regardful of thy quiet Rule,
Shall Fancy, Friendship, Science, smiling Peace
  Thy gentlest Influence own,
  And love thy fav'rite Name!

REV. WILLIAM GILPIN 1724–1804

from

LANDSCAPE PAINTING

Far up yon river, opening to the sea,
Just where the distant coast extends a curve,
A lengthened train of sea-fowl urge their flight.
Observe their files! In what exact array
The dark battalion floats, distinctly seen
Before yon silver cliff! Now, now, they reach
That lonely beacon; now are lost again
In yon dark cloud.   How pleasing is the sight!
The forest-glade from its wild, timorous herd,
Receives not richer ornament, than here
From birds this lonely sea-view.

REV. WILLIAM MASON 1724–1797

from

THE ENGLISH GARDEN

Yorkshire

Happy art thou if thou can'st call thine own
Such scenes as these: where Nature and where Time
Have work'd congenial; where a scatter'd host
Of antique oaks darken thy sidelong hills;
While, rushing thro' their branches, rifted cliffs
Dart their white heads, and glitter thro' the gloom.

16

More happy still, if one superior rock
Bear on its brow the shiver'd fragment huge
Of some old Norman fortress; happier far,
Ah, then most happy, if thy vale below
Wash, with the crystal coolness of its rills,
Some mouldring abbey's ivy-vested wall.

OLIVER GOLDSMITH 1728–1774

from
THE DESERTED VILLAGE

Sweet was the sound, when oft at evening's close
Up yonder hill the village murmur rose;
There, as I pass'd with careless steps and slow,
The mingling notes came soften'd from below;
The swain responsive as the milk-maid sung,
The sober herd that low'd to meet their young;
The noisy geese that gabbled o'er the pool,
The playful children just let loose from school;
The watchdog's voice that bay'd the whisp'ring wind,
And the loud laugh that spoke the vacant mind;
These all in sweet confusion sought the shade,
And fill'd each pause the nightingale had made.
But now the sounds of population fail,
No cheerful murmurs fluctuate in the gale,
No busy steps the grass-grown foot-way tread,
For all the bloomy flush of life is fled.
All but yon widow'd, solitary thing
That feebly bends beside the plashy spring;
She, wretched matron, forc'd, in age, for bread,
To strip the brook with mantling cresses spread,
To pick her wintry faggot from the thorn,
To seek her nightly shed, and weep till morn.

from

ODE TO A FRIEND ON HIS LEAVING
A FAVOURITE VILLAGE IN HAMPSHIRE

Ah, mourn, thou loved retreat! No more
Shall classic steps thy scenes explore!
When morn's pale rays but faintly peep
O'er yonder oak-crown'd airy steep,
Who now shall climb its brows to view
The length of landscape, ever new,
Where Summer flings, in careless pride,
Her varied vesture far and wide?
Who mark, beneath, each village-charm,
Or grange, or elm-encircled farm;
The flinty dovecote's crowded roof,
Watch'd by the kite that sails aloof;
The tufted pines, whose umbrage tall
Darkens the long-deserted hall;
The veteran beech, that on the plain
Collects at eve the playful train;
The cot that smokes with early fire,
The low-roof'd fane's embosom'd spire?
   Who now shall indolently stray
Through the deep forest's tangled way;
Pleased at his custom'd task to find
The well known hoary-tressed hind,
That toils with feeble hands to glean
Of wither'd boughs his pittance mean?
Who mid thy nooks of hazel sit,
Lost in some melancholy fit,
And listening to the raven's croak,
The distant flail, the falling oak?
Who, through the sunshine and the shower,
Descry the rainbow-painted tower?
Who, wandering at return of May,
Catch the first cuckoo's vernal lay?
Who musing waste the summer hour,
Where high o'er-arching trees embower

The grassy lane so rarely paced,
With azure flowerets idly graced?
Unnoticed now, at twilight's dawn
Returning reapers cross the lawn;
Nor fond attention loves to note
The wether's bell from folds remote:
While, own'd by no poetic eye,
Thy pensive evenings shade the sky!

JOHN CUNNINGHAM 1729–1773

A LANDSCAPE

Now that summer's ripen'd bloom
    Frolics where the winter frown'd,
Stretch'd upon these banks of broom,
    We command the landscape round.

Nature in the prospect yields
    Humble dales, and mountains bold,
Meadows, woodlands, heaths—and fields
    Yellow'd o'er with waving gold.

Goats upon that frowning steep,
    Fearless, with their kidlings brouse!
Here a flock of snowy sheep!
    There an herd of motley cows!

On the uplands, every glade
    Brightens in the blaze of day;
O'er the vales, the sober shade
    Softens to an evening grey.

Where the rill, by slow degrees,
    Swells into a crystal pool,
Shaggy rocks and shelving trees
    Shoot to keep the waters cool.

Shiver'd by a thunder-stroke,
  From the mountain's misty ridge,
O'er the brook a ruin'd oak,
  Near the farm-house, forms a bridge.

On her breast the sunny beam
  Glitters in meridian pride;
Yonder as the virgin stream
  Hastens to the restless tide:—

Where the ships by wanton gales
  Wafted, o'er the green waves run,
Sweet to see their swelling sails
  Whiten'd by the laughing sun!

High upon the daisied hill,
  Rising from the slope of trees,
How the wings of yonder mill
  Labour in the busy breeze!—

Cheerful as a summer's morn
  (Bouncing from her loaded pad)
Where the maid presents her corn,
  Smirking, to the miller's lad.

O'er the green a festal throng
  Gambols, in fantastic trim!
As the full cart moves along,
  Hearken—'tis their harvest hymn!

Linnets on the crowded sprays
  Chorus,—and the wood-larks rise
Soaring with a song of praise,
  'Till the sweet notes reach the skies.

Torrents in extended sheets
  Down the cliffs, dividing, break:
'Twixt the hills the water meets,
  Settling in a silver lake! . . .

Where the mantling willows nod,
　　From the green bank's slopy side,
Patient, with his well-thrown rod,
　　Many an angler breaks the tide!

On the isles, with osiers drest,
　　Many a fair-plum'd halcyon breeds!
Many a wild bird hides her nest,
　　Cover'd in yon crackling reeds.

Fork-tail'd prattlers as they pass
　　To their nestlings in the rock,
Daring on the liquid glass,
　　Seem to kiss the mimic'd flock. . .

Painted gardens—grots—and groves,
　　Intermingling shade and light!
Lengthen'd vistas, green alcoves,
　　Join to give the eye delight.

Hamlets—villages, and spires,
　　Scatter'd on the landscape lie,
'Till the distant view retires,
　　Closing in an azure sky.

JOHN CUNNINGHAM 1729–1773

from

DAY: A PASTORAL

EVENING

O'er the heath the heifer strays
　　Free;—(the furrow'd task is done)
Now the village windows blaze,
　　Burnish'd by the setting sun.

Now he hides behind the hill,
　　Sinking from a golden sky:
Can the pencil's mimic skill,
　　Copy the refulgent dye?

Trudging as the ploughmen go,
  (To the smoking hamlet bound)
Giant-like their shadows grow,
  Lengthen'd o'er the level ground.

Where the rising forest spreads,
  Shelter for the lordly dome!
To their high-built airy beds,
  See the rooks returning home!

As the lark with vary'd tune,
  Carols to the evening loud;
Mark the mild resplendent moon,
  Breaking through a parted cloud!

Now the hermit howlet peeps
  From the barn, or twisted brake:
And the blue mist slowly creeps,
  Curling on the silver lake.

As the trout in speckled pride,
  Playful from its bosom springs;
To the banks, a ruffled tide
  Verges in successive rings.

Tripping through the silken grass,
  O'er the path-divided dale,
Mark the rose-complexion'd lass,
  With her well-pois'd milking pail.

Linnets, with unnumber'd notes,
  And the cuckoo bird with two,
Tuning sweet their mellow throats,
  Bid the setting sun adieu.

from

AMWELL: A DESCRIPTIVE POEM

Hertfordshire

How picturesque
The slender group of airy elm, the clump
Of pollard oak, or ash, with ivy brown
Entwin'd; the walnut's gloomy breadth of boughs,
The orchard's ancient fence of rugged pales,
The haystack's dusky cone, the moss-grown shed,
The clay-built barn; the elder-shaded cot,
Whose white-wash'd gable prominent through green
Of waving branches shows, perchance inscrib'd
With some past owner's name, or rudely grac'd
With rustic dial, that scarcely serves to mark
Time's ceaseless flight; the wall with mantling vines
O'erspread, the porch with climbing woodbine wreath'd,
And under sheltering eaves the sunny bench
Where brown hives range, whose busy tenants fill,
With drowsy hum, the little garden gay,
Whence blooming beans, and spicy herbs, and flowers,
Exhale around a rich perfume! Here rests
The empty wain; there idle lies the plough:
By Summer's hand unharness'd, here the steed,
Short ease enjoying, crops the daisied lawn;
Here bleats the nursling lamb, the heifer there
Waits at the yard-gate lowing.

JOHN SCOTT 1730–1783

from

RURAL SCENERY—ECLOGUE I

Hertfordshire

Then soon gay summer brings his gaudy train,
His crimson poppies deck the corn-clad plain;
There scabious blue, and purple knapweed rise,
And weld and yarrow show their various dyes.

In shady lanes red foxglove bells appear,
And golden spikes the downy mulleins rear;
The inclosure ditch luxuriant mallows hide,
And branchy succory crowds the pathway side.

The autumnal fields few pleasing plants supply,
Save where pale eyebright grows in pastures dry,
Or vervain blue, for magic rites renown'd,
And in the village precincts only found.

Th' autumnal hedges withering leaves embrown,
Save where wild climbers spread their silvery down,
And rugged blackthornes bend with purple sloes,
And the green skewerwood seeds of scarlet shows . . .

Before my door the box-edg'd border lies,
Where flowers of mint and thyme and tansy rise;
Along my wall the yellow stonecrop grows,
And the red houseleek on my brown thatch blows.

Among green osiers winds my stream away,
Where the blue halcyon skims from spray to spray,
Where waves the bulrush as the waters glide,
And yellow flag-flow'rs deck the sunny side.

Spread o'er the slope of yon steep western hill,
My fruitful orchard shelters all the vill;
There pear-trees tall their tops aspiring show,
And apple-boughs their branches mix below.

East from my cottage stretch delightful meads,
Where rows of willows rise, and banks of reeds;
There roll clear rivers; there, old elms between,
The mill's white roof and circling wheels are seen. . .

How that bright landscape lures the eye to gaze,
Where with his beams the distant windows blaze!
And the gilt vane, high on the steeple spire,
Glows in the air—a dazzling spot of fire!

Behind yon hill he now forsakes our sight,
And yon tall beeches catch his latest light;
The hamlet smokes in amber wreaths arise;
White mist, like water, on the valley lies.

WILLIAM COWPER 1731–1800

from

THE TASK—Book I

Buckinghamshire

Now roves the eye;
And, posted on this speculative height,
Exults in its command. The sheep-fold here
Pours out its fleecy tenants o'er the glebe.
At first, progressive as a stream, they seek
The middle field; but, scatter'd by degrees,
Each to his choice, soon whiten all the land.
There from the sun-burnt hay-field, homeward creeps
The loaded wain; while, lighten'd of its charge,
The wain that meets it passes swiftly by;
The boorish driver leaning o'er his team
Vocif'rous, and impatient of delay.
Nor less attractive is the woodland scene,
Diversified with trees of ev'ry growth,
Alike, yet various. Here the gray smooth trunks
Of ash, or lime, or beech, distinctly shine,
Within the twilight of their distant shades;
There, lost behind a rising ground, the wood
Seems sunk, and shorten'd to its topmost boughs.
No tree in all the grove but has its charms,
Though each its hue peculiar; paler some,
And of a wannish gray; the willow such,
And poplar, that with silver lines his leaf,
And ash far-stretching his umbrageous arm;
Of deeper green the elm; and deeper still,
Lord of the woods, the long-surviving oak.
Some glossy-leav'd, and shining in the sun,
The maple, and the beech of oily nuts
Prolific, and the lime at dewy eve
Diffusing odours: nor unnoted pass

25

The sycamore, capricious in attire,
Now green, now tawny, and, ere autumn yet
Have chang'd the woods, in scarlet honours bright.
O'er these, but far beyond (a spacious map
Of hill and valley interpos'd between),
The Ouse, dividing the well-water'd land,
Now glitters in the sun, and now retires,
As bashful, yet impatient to be seen.

from

THE TASK—Book V

Buckinghamshire

'Tis morning; and the sun, with ruddy orb
Ascending, fires th' horizon: while the clouds,
That crowd away before the driving wind,
More ardent as the disk emerges more,
Resemble most some city in a blaze,
Seen through the leafless wood. His slanting ray
Slides ineffectual down the snowy vale,
And, tinging all with his own rosy hue,
From ev'ry herb and ev'ry spiry blade
Stretches a length of shadow o'er the field.
Mine, spindling into longitude immense,
In spite of gravity, and sage remark
That I myself am but a fleeting shade,
Provokes me to a smile. With eye askance
I view the muscular proportion'd limb
Transform'd to a lean shank. The shapeless pair
As they design'd to mock me, at my side
Take step for step; and, as I near approach
The cottage, walk along the plaster'd wall,
Prepost'rous sight! the legs without the man.
The verdure of the plain lies buried deep
Beneath the dazzling deluge; and the bents
And coarser grass, upspearing o'er the rest,
Of late unsightly and unseen, now shine
Conspicuous, and, in bright apparel clad
And fledg'd with icy feathers, nod superb.

Carmarthenshire

Gromgar Hill

The cattle mourn in corners, where the fence
Screens them, and seem half petrified to sleep
In unrecumbent sadness. There they wait
Their wonted fodder; not like hung'ring man,
Fretful if unsupply'd; but silent, meek,
And patient of the slow-pac'd swain's delay.
He from the stack carves out th' accustom'd load,
Deep-plunging, and again deep-plunging oft,
His broad keen knife into the solid mass:
Smooth as a wall the upright remnant stands,
With such undeviating and even force
He severs it away: no needless care,
Lest storms should overset the leaning pile
Deciduous, or its own unbalanc'd weight.
Forth goes the woodman, leaving unconcern'd
The cheerful haunts of man; to wield the axe
And drive the wedge, in yonder forest drear,
From morn to eve his solitary task.
Shaggy, and lean, and shrewd, with pointed ears
And tail cropp'd short, half lurcher and half cur,
His dog attends him. Close behind his heel
Now creeps he slow; and now, with many a frisk
Wide-scamp'ring, snatches up the drifted snow
With iv'ry teeth, or ploughs it with his snout;
Then shakes his powder'd coat, and barks for joy.
Heedless of all his pranks, the sturdy churl
Moves right toward the mark; nor stops for aught,
But now and then with pressure of his thumb
T'adjust the fragrant charge of a short tube,
That fumes beneath his nose: the trailing cloud
Streams far behind him, scenting all the air.

from
THE TASK—Book VI
Buckinghamshire

The night was winter in his roughest mood;
The morning sharp and clear. But now at noon
Upon the southern side of the slant hills,
And where the woods fence off the northern blast,

The season smiles, resigning all its rage,
And has the warmth of May. The vault is blue
Without a cloud, and white without a speck
The dazzling splendour of the scene below.
Again the harmony comes o'er the vale;
And through the trees I view th' embattled tow'r,
Whence all the music. I again perceive
The soothing influence of the wafted strains,
And settle in soft musings as I tread
The walk, still verdant, under oaks and elms,
Whose outspread branches overarch the glade.
The roof, though movable through all its length
As the wind sways it, has yet well suffic'd,
And, intercepting in their silent fall
The frequent flakes, has kept a path for me.
No noise is here, or none that hinders thought.
The redbreast warbles still, but is content
With slender notes, and more than half suppress'd:
Pleas'd with his solitude, and flitting light
From spray to spray, where'er he rests he shakes
From many a twig the pendent drops of ice,
That tinkle in the wither'd leaves below.

WILLIAM COWPER 1731–1800

THE POPLAR FIELD

Buckinghamshire

The poplars are fell'd, farewell to the shade
And the whispering sound of the cool colonnade,
The winds play no longer, and sing in the leaves,
Nor Ouse on his bosom their image receives.

Twelve years have elaps'd since I first took a view
Of my favourite field and the bank where they grew,
And now in the grass behold they are laid,
And the tree is my seat that once lent me a shade.

The blackbird has fled to another retreat
Where the hazels afford him a screen from the heat,
And the scene where his melody charm'd me before,
Resounds with his sweet-flowing ditty no more.

My fugitive years are all hasting away,
And I must ere long lie as lowly as they,
With a turf on my breast, and a stone at my head,
Ere another such grove shall arise in its stead.

'Tis a sight to engage me, if anything can,
To muse on the perishing pleasures of man;
Though his life be a dream, his enjoyments, I see,
Have a being less durable even than he.

LORD THURLOW 1731–1806

ON BEHOLDING BODIAM CASTLE

Sussex

O thou, brave ruin of the passed time,
   When glorious spirits shone in burning arms,
   And the brave trumpet, with its sweet alarms,
Call'd *honour!* at the matin hour sublime,
And the grey ev'ning: thou hast had thy prime,
   And thy full vigour, and the eating harms
   Of age have robb'd thee of thy warlike charms,
And placed thee here, an image in my rhyme;
   The owl now haunts thee, and, oblivion's plant,
The creeping ivy, has o'er-veil'd thy towers;
   And Rother, looking up with eye askant,
Recalling to his mind thy brighter hours,
   Laments the time, when, fair and elegant,
Beauty first laugh'd from out thy joyous bowers!

JAMES BEATTIE 1735–1803

from

THE MINSTREL

Aberdeen

And oft he traced the uplands, to survey,
When o'er the sky advanced the kindling dawn,
The crimson cloud, blue main, and mountain grey,
And lake, dim-gleaming on the smoky lawn:

Far to the west the long, long vale withdrawn,
Where twilight loves to linger for a while;
And now he faintly kens the bounding fawn,
And villager abroad at early toil.
But, lo! the Sun appears! and heaven, earth, ocean, smile. . .

The cottage curs at early pilgrim bark;
Crowned with her pail the tripping milkmaid sings;
The whistling ploughman stalks afield; and, hark!
Down the rough slope the ponderous waggon rings;
Thro' rustling corn the hare astonished springs;
Slow tolls the village clock the drowsy hour;
The partridge bursts away on whirring wings;
Deep mourns the turtle in sequestered bower,
And shrill lark carols clear from her aërial tour.

REV. WILLIAM CROWE 1745–1829

from

LEWESDON HILL

Dorset

From this proud eminence on all sides round
Th'unbroken prospect opens to my view,
On all sides large; save only where the head
Of Pillesdon rises, Pillesdon's lofty Pen:
So call (still rendering to his ancient name
Observance due) that rival Height south-west,
Which, like a rampire, bounds the vale beneath.
There woods, there blooming orchards, there are seen
Herds ranging, or at rest beneath the shade
Of some wide-branching oak; there goodly fields
Of corn, and verdant pasture, whence the kine,
Returning with their milky treasure home,
Store the rich dairy; such fair plenty fills
The pleasant vale of Marshwood, pleasant now,
Since that the Spring hath deck'd anew the meads
With flowery vesture, and the warmer sun
Their foggy moistness drain'd; in wintry days
Cold, vapourish, miry, wet, and to the flocks

Unfriendly, when autumnal rains begin
To drench the spungy turf; but ere that time
The careful shepherd moves to healthier soil,
Rechasing, lest his tender ewes should coath
In the dank pasturage. Yet not the fields
Of Evesham, nor that ample valley named
Of the White Horse, its antique monument
Carved in the chalky bourne, for beauty and wealth
Might equal, though surpassing in extent,
This fertile vale, in length from Lewesdon's base
Extended to the sea, and water'd well
By many a rill; but chief with thy clear stream,
Thou nameless Rivulet, who, from the side
Of Lewesdon softly welling forth, dost trip
Adown the valley, wandering sportively. . .

How is it vanish'd in a hasty spleen,
The Tor of Glastonbury! Even but now
I saw the hoary pile cresting the top
Of that north-western hill; and in this Now
A cloud hath pass'd on it, and its dim bulk
Becomes annihilate, or if not, a spot
Which the strained vision tires itself to find.

REV. SAMUEL JACKSON PRATT 1749–1814

from
COTTAGE PICTURES

No village dames and maidens now are seen,
But madams, and the misses of the green!
Farm-house, and farm too, are in deep disgrace,
'Tis now the lodge, the cottage, or the place!
Or if a farm, *ferme ornee* is the phrase!
And if a cottage, of these modern days,
Expect no more to see the straw-built shed,
But a fantastic villa in its stead!
Pride, thinly veiled in mock humility;
The name of cot, without its poverty!
By affectation, still with thatching crowned;
By affectation, still with ivy bound;

By affectation, still the mantling vine
The door-way and the window-frames entwine;
The hawthorn bow'rs, and benches near the grove,
Give place to temples, and the rich alcove:
A naked Venus here, a Bacchus there,
And mimic ruins, kept in good repair;
The real rustic's sweet and simple bounds,
Quick-set and garden, changed to pleasure-grounds,
And the fresh sod, that formed the pathway green,
The strawberry bed, and currant-bush between
The honey-suckle hedge and lily tall,
Yield to the shrubbery and high-raised wall;
Then for exotics of botanic fame,
Of which the lady scarcely knows the name;
Yet, as with country friend she goes the round,
She christens them with words of learned sound.
The wall, in foreign fruits so rich and fine,
Forms the dessert, when farmer-gentry dine!
And then for water! geese and ducks no more
Have leave to puddle round a modern door;
Fair on the glassy lake they sail in state,
And seem to know a prouder change of fate;
From thence, on china served, they grace the dish,
And vie in honours with the silver fish.

CHARLOTTE SMITH 1749–1806

from

BEACHY HEAD

Sussex

Where woods of ash, and beech,
And partial copses, fringe the green hill foot,
The upland shepherd rears his modest home;
There wanders by a little nameless stream
That from the hill wells forth, bright now and clear,
Or after rain with chalky mixture grey,
But still refreshing in its shallow course
The cottage garden; most for use design'd,

Yet not of beauty destitute. The vine
Mantles the little casement; yet the briar
Drops fragrant dew among the July flowers;
And pansies ray'd, and freak'd and mottled pinks
Grow among balm, and rosemary and rue;
There honeysuckles flaunt, and roses blow
Almost uncultur'd: some with dark green leaves
Contrast their flowers of pure unsullied white;
Others like velvet robes of regal state
Of richest crimson; while, in thorny moss
Enshrin'd and cradled, the most lovely wear
The hues of youthful beauty's glowing cheek. —
With fond regret I recollect e'en now
In Spring and Summer what delight I felt
Among these cottage gardens, and how much
Such artless nosegays, knotted with a rush
By village housewife or her ruddy maid,
Were welcome to me; soon and simply pleas'd,
An early worshipper atNature's shrine,
I lov'd her rudest scenes—warrens, and heaths,
And yellow commons, and birch-shaded hollows,
And hedgerows, bordering unfrequented lanes
Bower'd with wild roses, and the clasping woodbine,
Where purple tassles of the tangling vetch
With bittersweet and bryony inweave,
And the dew fills the silver bindweed's cups—
I lov'd to trace the brooks whose humid banks
Nourish the harebell, and the freckled pagil;
And stroll among o'ershadowing woods of beech,
Lending in summer from the heats of noon
A whispering shade; while haply there reclines
Some pensive lover of uncultur'd flowers,
Who from the tumps, with bright green mosses clad,
Plucks the wood-sorrel with its light thin leaves,
Heart-shap'd and triply-folded, and its root
Creeping like beaded coral; or who there
Gathers, the copse's pride, anemones,
With rays like golden studs on ivory laid
Most delicate: but touch'd with purple clouds,
Fit crown for April's fair but changeful brow.

ON A WET SUMMER

Devon

All ye, who far from town, in rural hall,
Like me, were wont to dwell near pleasant field,
Enjoying all the sunny day did yield,
   With me the change lament, in irksome thrall,
By rains incessant held; for now no call
   From early swain invites my hand to wield
   The scythe; in parlour dim I sit conceal'd,
And mark the lessening sand from hour-glass fall;
   Or 'neath my window view the wistful train
Of dripping poultry, whom the vine's broad leaves
   Shelter no more.—Mute is the mournful plain,
     Silent the swallow sits beneath the thatch,
     And vacant hind hangs pensive o'er his hatch,
Counting the frequent drop from reeded eaves.

REV. GEORGE CRABBE 1754–1832

from

THE BOROUGH—Letter II

Suffolk

But ere you enter, yon bold Tower survey,
Tall and entire, and venerably grey,
For time has soften'd what was harsh when new,
And now the stains are all of sober hue;
The living stains which Nature's hand alone,
Profuse of life, pours forth upon the stone:
For ever growing; where the common eye
Can but the bare and rocky bed descry;
There Science loves to trace her tribes minute,
The juiceless foliage, and the tasteless fruit;
There she perceives then round the surface creep,
And while they meet their due distinction keep;
Mix'd but not blended; each its name retains,
And these are Nature's ever-during stains . . . .

34

Seeds, to our eye invisible, will find
On the rude rock the bed that fits their kind;
There, in the rugged soil, they safely dwell,
Till showers and snows the subtle atoms swell,
And spread th'enduring foliage;—then we trace
The freckled flower upon the flinty base;
These all increase, till in unnoticed years
The stony tower as grey with age appears;
With coats of vegetation, thinly spread,
Coat above coat, the living on the dead:
These then dissolve to dust, and make a way
For bolder foliage, nursed by their decay:
The long-enduring ferns in time will all
Die and depose their dust upon the wall;
Where the wing'd seed may rest, till many a flower
Show Flora's triumph o'er the falling tower.

REV. GEORGE CRABBE 1754–1832

from

TALES

X—The Lover's Journey

Suffolk

When next appear'd a *dam*—so call the place—
Where lies a road confined in narrow space;
A work of labour, for on either side
Is level fen, a prospect wild and wide,
With dikes on either hand by ocean's self supplied:
Far on the right the distant sea is seen,
And salt the springs that feed the marsh between;
Beneath an ancient bridge, the straiten'd flood
Rolls through its sloping banks of slimy mud;
Near it a sunken boat resists the tide,
That frets and hurries to th' opposing side;
The rushes sharp, that on the borders grow,
Bend their brown flow'rets to the stream below,
Impure in all its course, in all its progress slow:
Here a grave Flora scarcely deigns to bloom,
Nor wears a rosy blush, nor sheds perfume;

35

The few dull flowers that o'er the place are spread
Partake the nature of their fenny bed;
Here on its wiry stem, in rigid bloom,
Grows the salt lavender that lacks perfume;
Here the dwarf sallows creep, the septfoil harsh,
And the soft slimy mallow of the marsh;
Low on the ear the distant billows sound,
And just in view appears their stony bound;
No hedge nor tree conceals the glowing sun,
Birds, save a wat'ry tribe, the district shun,
Nor chirp among the reeds where bitter waters run.

from

TALES

V—The Patron

Suffolk

Cold grew the foggy morn, the day was brief,
Loose on the cherry hung the crimson leaf;
The dew dwelt ever on the herb; the woods
Roar'd with strong blasts, with mighty showers the floods;
All green was vanish'd, save of pine and yew,
That still displayed their melancholy hue;
Save the green holly with its berries red,
And the green moss that o'er the gravel spread.

REV. GEORGE CRABBE 1754–1832

TALES OF THE HALL

XIII—Delay has Danger

Suffolk

But now dejected, languid, listless, low,
He saw the wind upon the water blow,
And the cold stream curl'd onward as the gale
From the pine-hill blew harshly down the dale;
On the right side the youth a wood survey'd
With all its dark intensity of shade;

Far to the left he saw the huts of men,
Half hid in mist that hung upon the fen;
Before him swallows gathering for the sea
Took their short flights and twitter'd on the lea;
And near the bean-sheaf stood, the harvest done,
And slowly blacken'd in the sickly sun;
All these were sad in nature, or they took
Sadness from him, the likeness of his look.

from

TALES OF THE HALL

Book XX—The Cathedral-Walk

Suffolk

'In an autumnal evening, cool and still,
The sun just dropp'd beneath a distant hill,
The children gazing on the quiet scene,
Then rose in glory night's majestic queen;
And pleasant was the checker'd light and shade
Her golden beams and maple shadows made;
An ancient tree that in the garden grew,
And that fair picture on the gravel threw.
    Then all was silent, save the sounds that make
Silence more awful, while they faintly break;
The frighten'd bat's low shriek, the beetle's hum,
With nameless sounds we know not whence they come.
    Such was the evening; and that ancient seat
The scene where then some neighbours chanced to meet;
Up to the door led broken steps of stone,
Whose dewy surface in the moonlight shone,
On vegetation, that with progress slow,
Where man forbears to fix his foot, will grow;
The window's depth and dust repell'd the ray
Of the moon's light and of the setting day.

from

POSTHUMOUS TALES

X—The Ancient Mansion

Suffolk

These very pinnacles, and turrets small,
And windows dim, have beauty in them all.
How stately stand yon pines upon the hill,
How soft the murmurs of that living rill,
And o'er the park's tall paling, scarcely higher,
Peeps the low church and shows the modest spire.
Unnumber'd violets on those banks appear,
And all the first-born beauties of the year.
The grey-green blossoms of the willow bring
The large wild bees upon the labouring wing.
Then comes the Summer with augmented pride,
Whose pure small streams along the valleys glide:
Her richer Flora their brief charms display;
And, as the fruit advances, fall away.
Then shall th'autumnal yellow clothe the leaf,
What time the reaper binds the burden'd sheaf:
Then silent groves denote the dying year,
The morning frost, and noon-tide gossamer;
And all be silent in the scene around,
All save the distant sea's uncertain sound,
Or here and there the gun whose loud report
Proclaims to man that Death is but his sport:
And then the wintry winds begin to blow,
Then fall the flaky stars of gathering snow,
When on the thorn the ripening sloe, yet blue,
Takes the bright varnish of the morning dew;
The aged moss grows brittle on the pale,
The dry boughs splinter in the windy gale,
And every changing season of the year
Stamps on the scene its English character.

from

WALKS IN A FOREST

Summer—Noon

Staffordshire

On the bank worn bare,
And printed with ten thousand steps, the colts
In shifting groups combine; or, to the brink
Descending, dip their pasterns in the wave.
Bolder the horned tribes, or less of heat
And teasing insects patient, far from shore
Immerge their chests; and while the hungry swarm
Now soars aloof, now resolute descends,
Lash their tormented sides; and, stamping quick
And oft, the muddy fluid scatter round.
Fix'd many an hour, till milder skies recall
Desire of long forgotten food, they stand
Each in its place; save when some wearied beast
The pressure of the crowd no longer brooks,
Or in mere vagrant mood her station quits
Restless; or some intruder, from afar
Flying o'er hill and plain the gadbee's sting,
(For still the dreaded hum she hears, and shakes
The air with iterated lowings,) spies
The wat'ry gleam. With wildly-tossing head,
And tail projected far, and maddening gait,
She plunges in, and breaks the ranks, and spreads
Confusion, till constrain'd at length she stops,
Wedged in the throng.

from

WALKS IN A FOREST

Winter—Thaw

Staffordshire

The fleecy mantle which of late conceal'd
The lawns, and burying deep the furzy brake
Display'd, upheav'd in undulating mounds,
A rude resemblance of the forms below,
Is vanish'd. From the south dissolving gales
Blew: the snows felt their influence. In the woods,
Humid and comfortless, from dawn to eve
Were heard incessant drippings, pattering loud
When the air moved the branches. The soft mass
Beneath of every drop the impression took,
Pierced into hollows numerous as the cells
That hide the golden treasures of the bee.
Oft, from its lodgement on the forked bough
Sliding, a snowy heap with leaden sound
Sunk buried in the unresisting floor.
Soon through the lessening weight the elastic gorse
Its sullen shoots, by contrast darker, push'd.
Soon on the level plain green spots emerged,
Where raised the busy ant or delving mole
Its subterranean dwelling; sloppy pools
In the surrounding pulp lay stagnant. Streams
From each low bank ran trickling; while above,
The new-born currents, pouring from the hills,
O'er the smooth slopes in brown diffusion stray'd,
Or deep in echoing gullies roar'd unseen.

from

WALKS IN A FOREST

Winter—Frost

Staffordshire

Sunk in the vale, whose concave depth receives
The waters draining from their shelvy banks
When the shower beats, yon pool with pallid gleam
Betrays its icy covering. From the glade
Issuing in pensive file, and moving slow,
The cattle, all unwitting of the change,
To quench their customary thirst advance.
With wondering stare and fruitless search they trace
The solid margin: now bend low the head
In act to drink; now with fastidious nose
Snuffing the marble floor, and breathing loud,
From the cold touch withdraw. Awhile they stand
In disappointment mute; with ponderous feet
Then bruise the surface: to each stroke the woods
Reply; forth gushes the imprison'd wave.

REV. WILLIAM LISLE BOWLES 1762–1850

AVENUE IN SAVERNAKE FOREST

Wiltshire

How soothing sound the gentle airs that move
The innumerable leaves, high overhead,
When autumn first, from the long avenue,
That lifts its arching height of ancient shade,
Steals here and there a leaf!
               Within the gloom,
In partial sunshine white, some trunks appear,
Studding the glens of fern; in solemn shade
Some mingle their dark branches, but yet all,
All make a sad sweet music, as they move,
Not undelightful to a stranger's heart.

They seem to say, in accents audible,
Farewell to summer, and farewell the strains
Of many a lithe and feathered chorister,
That through the depth of these incumbent woods
Made the long summer gladsome.
                            I have heard
To the deep-mingling sounds of organs clear,
(When slow the choral anthem rose beneath),
The glimmering minster, through its pillared aisles,
Echo;—but not more sweet the vaulted roof
Rang to those linked harmonies, than here
The high wood answers to the lightest breath
Of nature.

REV. WILLIAM LISLE BOWLES 1762–1850

from

SKETCH FROM BOWDEN HILL
AFTER SICKNESS

Somerset

                            Upon the point
Of the descending steep I stand.
                            How rich,
How mantling in the gay and gorgeous tints
Of summer! far beneath me, sweeping on,
From field to field, from vale to cultured vale,
The prospect spreads its crowded beauties wide!
Long lines of sunshine, and of shadow, streak
The farthest distance; where the passing light
Alternate falls, 'mid undistinguished trees,
White dots of gleamy domes, and peeping towers,
As from the painter's instant touch, appear.
    As thus the eye ranges from hill to hill,
Here white with passing sunshine, there with trees
Innumerable shaded, clustering more,
As the long vale retires, the ample scene,
Warm with new grace and beauty, seems to live. . .
From yonder line, where fade the farthest hills
Which bound the blue lap of the swelling vale,

At Lewknor

Oxfordshire

On whose last line, seen like a beacon, hangs
Thy tower, benevolent, accomplished Hoare,
To where I stand, how wide the interval!
Yet instantaneous, to the hurrying eye
Displayed; though peeping towers and villages
Thick scattered, 'mid the intermingling elms,
And towns remotely marked by hovering smoke,
And grass-green pastures with their herds, and seats
Of rural beauty, cottages and farms,
Unnumbered as the hedgerows, lie between!

REV. WILLIAM LISLE BOWLES 1762–1850

THE SHEPHERD AND HIS DOG
Wiltshire

My dog and I are both grown old;
    On these wild downs we watch all day;
He looks in my face when the wind blows cold,
    And thus methinks I hear him say:

The gray stone circlet is below,
    The village smoke is at our feet;
We nothing hear but the sailing crow,
    And wandering flocks, that roam and bleat.

Far off, the early horseman hies,
    In shower or sunshine rushing on;
Yonder the dusty whirlwind flies;
    The distant coach is seen and gone.

Though solitude around is spread,
    Master, alone thou shalt not be;
And when the turf is on thy head,
    I only shall remember thee!

I marked his look of faithful care,
    I placed my hand on his shaggy side;
There is a sun that shines above,
    A sun that shines on both, I cried.

THE GLOW-WORM

Oh, what is this which shines so bright,
  And in the lonely place
Hangs out his small green lamp at night,
  The dewy bank to grace!

It is a glow-worm, still and pale
  It shines the whole night long,
When only stars, O nightingale,
  Seem listening to thy song!

And so amid the world's cold night,
  Through good report or ill,
Shines out the humble Christian's light,
  As lonely and as still.

SAMUEL ROGERS 1763–1855

A WISH

Mine be a cot beside the hill,
  A bee-hive's hum shall soothe my ear;
A willowy brook, that turns a mill,
  With many a fall shall linger near.

The swallow, oft, beneath my thatch,
  Shall twitter from her clay-built nest;
Oft shall the pilgrim lift the latch,
  And share my meal, a welcome guest.

Around my ivy'd porch shall spring
  Each fragrant flower that drinks the dew;
And Lucy, at her wheel, shall sing
  In russet gown and apron blue.

The village church, among the trees,
  Where first our marriage-vows were given,
With merry peals shall swell the breeze,
  And point with taper spire to heaven.

from

THE VILLAGE CURATE

Oxfordshire

Then let the village bells, as often wont,
Come swelling on the breeze, and to the sun,
Half-set, sing merrily their ev'ning song.
I ask not for the cause—it matters not.
It is enough for me to hear the sound
Of the remote exhilarating peal,
Now dying all away, now faintly heard,
And now with loud and musical relapse
Its mellow changes huddling on the ear.
So have I stood at eve on Isis' banks,
To hear the merry Christ-Church bells rejoice.
So have I sat too in thy honour'd shades,
Distinguish'd Magdalen, on Cherwell's brink,
To hear thy silver Wolsey tones so sweet.
And so too have I paus'd and held my oar,
And suffered the slow stream to bear me home,
While Wykeham's peal along the meadow ran.

REV. JAMES HURDIS 1763–1801

from

A LANDSCAPE

Sussex

Behold that vale, whose sides are cloth'd with wood;
And here and there a pleasurable spot
Of intersected pasture, with its stack,
Cottage and lodge, few sheep, and grazing cow:
Mark how it mellows as it steals away,
And mingles fainter shadows, softer woods.
How gracefully it parts, and winds along,
To leave that rising ground, on whose fresh top
Above the green enclosures stands a Church,
Which smiles with glory as the ev'ning sun,

45

And seems to love the prospect it adorns.
Behold behind it, as the vale recedes
And falls into a flat the eye scarce sees,
A family of hills, some near, some far,
Withdrawing till their faint expiring tops
Are almost lost, and melted into air.

REV. JAMES HURDIS 1763–1801

from

THE VILLAGE CURATE

Sussex

    I love to meet
A sudden turn like this, which stops me short,
Extravagantly devious, and invites
Or up the hill or down; then winds again,
By reeling drunkard trod, and sudden ends
In a green swarded wain-way, not unlike
Cathedral aisle completely roof'd with boughs,
Which stretching up-hill through the gloomy wood
Displays at either end a giant door
Wide open'd.

REV. JAMES GRAHAME 1765–1811

from

THE SABBATH

Scottish Lowlands

    How still the morning of the hallow'd day!
Mute is the voice of rural labour, hush'd
The ploughboy's whistle, and the milkmaid's song.
The scythe lies glittering in the dewy wreath
Of tedded grass, mingled with fading flowers,
That yester-morn bloom'd waving in the breeze:
Sounds the most faint attract the ear—the hum
Of early bee, the trickling of the dew,
The distant bleating, midway up the hill.
Calmness sits thron'd on yon unmoving cloud.

To him who wanders o'er the upland leas,
The blackbird's note comes mellower from the dale;
And sweeter from the sky the gladsome lark
Warbles his heaven-tuned song; the lulling brook
Murmurs more gently down the deep-worn glen;
While from yon lowly roof, whose curling smoke
O'ermounts the mist, is heard, at intervals,
The voice of psalms, the simple song of praise.
    With dove-like wings, Peace o'er yon village broods:
The dizzying mill-wheel rests; the anvil's din
Hath ceased; all, all around is quietness.
Less fearful on this day, the limping hare
Stops, and looks back, and stops, and looks on man,
Her deadliest foe. The toil-worn horse, set free,
Unheedful of the pasture, roams at large;
And, as his stiff unwieldly bulk he rolls,
His iron-arm'd hoofs gleam in the morning-ray.

REV. JAMES GRAHAME 1765–1811

THE WILD DUCK AND HER BROOD

How calm that little lake! no breath of wind
Sighs through the reeds; a clear abyss it seems
Held in the concave of the inverted sky,—
In which is seen the rook's dull flagging wing
Move o'er the silvery clouds. How peaceful sails
Yon little fleet, the wild duck and her brood!
Fearless of harm, they row their easy way;
The water-lily, 'neath the plumy prows,
Dips, re-appearing in their·dimpled track.
Yet, even amid that scene of peace, the noise
Of war, unequal, dastard war, intrudes.
Yon revel rout of men, and boys, and dogs,
Boisterous approach; the spaniel dashes in;
Quick he descries the prey, and faster swims,
And eager barks: the harmless flock, dismayed,
Hasten to gain the thickest grove of reeds,
All but the parent pair; they, floating, wait
To lure the foe, and lead him from their young;

47

But soon themselves are forced to seek the shore.
Vain then the buoyant wing; the leaden storm
Arrests their flight; they, fluttering, bleeding fall,
And tinge the troubled bosom of the lake.

ROBERT BLOOMFIELD 1766–1825

from

THE FARMER'S BOY

Suffolk

Wide o'er the fields, in rising moisture strong,
Shoots up the simple flower, or creeps along
The mellow'd soil; imbibing fairer hues,
Or sweets from frequent showers and evening dews;
That summon from their shed the slumb'ring plows,
While health impregnates every breeze that blows.
No wheels support the diving, pointed share;
No groaning ox is doom'd to labour there; . . .
But, unassisted through each toilsome day,
With smiling brow the plowman cleaves his way,
Draws his fresh parallels, and, wid'ning still,
Treads slow the heavy dale, or climbs the hill:
Strong on the wing his busy followers play,
Where writhing earth-worms meet th' unwelcome day;
Till all is chang'd, and hill and level down
Assume a livery of sober brown.

JOHN HOOKHAM FRERE 1769–1846

MODERN IMPROVEMENTS

The cumbrous pollards that o'ershade,
    Those uplands rough with brakes and thorns,
The green way with its track-worn glade,
    The solitary grange forlorn,
The lonely pastures wild and drear,
    The lonely dwellings wide apart,
Are whispering to the fancy's ear
    A secret strain that moves the heart.

No forms of grandeur or of grace,
   In the rude landscape you behold,
But their rough lineaments retrace
   The features of the times of old:
They speak of customs long retained,
   Of simple, plain, primeval life,
They mark the little we have gained,
   With all our study, toil and strife:
Such England was to Shakespeare's eyes,
   So Chaucer viewed her as he roved,
In russet weeds of rustic guise,
   In homelier beauty more beloved.
Our ancient halls have left the land,
   Turrets and towers have passed away,
Arcades and porticoes were planned
   And these again have had their day:
Impatient, peevish wealth recalls
   The forms which she defaced before,
Unthrifty sires destroyed the halls
   Which modern prodigals restore;
Confounding England, Rome, and Greece,
   Each ancient and each modern race,
We dislocate with wild caprice
   All unities of time and place:
Yet here attended by the Muse
   Let harassed Fancy pause awhile
And unpolluted yet peruse
   This remnant of our ancient isle.

WILLIAM WORDSWORTH 1770–1850

from

THE RECLUSE

Westmorland

Embrace me then, ye Hills, and close me in;
Now in the clear and open day I feel
Your guardianship; I take it to my heart;
'Tis like the solemn shelter of the night.

But I would call thee beautiful, for mild,
And soft, and gay, and beautiful thou art
Dear Valley, having in thy face a smile
Though peaceful, full of gladness. Thou art pleased,
Pleased with thy crags and woody steeps, thy Lake,
Its one green island and its winding shores;
The multitude of little rocky hills,
Thy Church and cottages of mountain stone
Clustered like stars some few, but single most,
And lurking dimly in their shy retreats,
Or glancing at each other cheerful looks
Like separated stars with clouds between.
What want we? Have we not perpetual streams,
Warm woods, and sunny hills, and fresh green fields,
And mountains not less green, and flocks and herds,
And thickets full of songsters, and the voice
Of lordly birds, an unexpected sound
Heard now and then from morn to latest eve,
Admonishing the man who walks below
Of solitude and silence in the sky?
These have we, and a thousand nooks of earth
Have also these, but nowhere else is found,
Nowhere (or is it fancy?) can be found
The one sensation that is here; 'tis here,
Here as it found its way into my heart
In childhood, here as it abides by day,
By night, here only; or in chosen minds
That take it with them hence, where'er they go.
—'Tis, but I cannot name it, 'tis the sense
Of majesty, and beauty, and repose,
A blended holiness of earth and sky,
Something that makes this individual spot,
This small abiding place of many men,
A termination, and a last retreat,
A centre, come from wheresoe'er you will,
A whole without dependence or defect,
Made for itself, and happy in itself,
Perfect Contentment, Unity entire.

   Bleak season was it, turbulent and bleak,
When hitherward we journeyed side by side

Through burst of sunshine and through flying showers;
Paced the long vales—how long they were—and yet
How fast that length of way was left behind,
Wensley's rich Vale, and Sedbergh's naked heights.
The frosty wind, as if to make amends
For its keen breath, was aiding to our steps,
And drove us onward like two ships at sea,
Or like two birds, companions in mid-air,
Parted and reunited by the blast.
    Stern was the face of nature; we rejoiced
In that stern countenance, for our souls thence drew
A feeling of their strength. The naked trees,
The icy brooks, as on we passed, appeared
To question us. 'Whence come ye, to what end?'
They seemed to say, 'What would ye?', said the shower,
'Wild Wanderers, whither through my dark domain?'
The sunbeam said, 'Be happy'. When this vale
We entered, bright and solemn was the sky
That faced us with a passionate welcoming,
And led us to our threshold. Daylight failed
Insensibly, and round us gently fell
Composing darkness, with a quiet load
Of full contentment, in a little shed
Disturbed, uneasy in itself as seemed,
And wondering at its new inhabitants.
It loves us now, this Vale so beautiful
Begins to love us! by a sullen storm,
Two months unwearied of severest storm,
It put the temper of our minds to proof,
And found us faithful through the gloom, and heard
The poet mutter his prelusive songs
With cheerful heart, an unknown voice of joy
Among the silence of the woods and hills;
Silent to any gladsomeness of sound
With all their shepherds.

from

GUILT AND SORROW

Wiltshire

All, all was cheerless to the horizon's bound;
The weary eye—which, wheresoe'er it strays,
Marks nothing but the red suns's setting round,
Or on the earth strange lines, in former days
Left by gigantic arms—at length surveys
What seems an antique castle spreading wide;
Hoary and naked are its walls, and raise
Their brow sublime: in shelter there to bide
He turned, while rain poured down smoking on every side.

Pile of Stone-henge! so proud to hint yet keep
Thy secrets, thou that lov'st to stand and hear
The Plain resounding to the whirlwind's sweep,
Inmate of lonesome Nature's endless year;
Even if thou saw'st the giant wicker rear
For sacrifice its throngs of living men,
Before thy face did ever wretch appear,
Who in his heart had groaned with deadlier pain
Than he who, tempest-driven, thy shelter now would gain?

Within that fabric of mysterious form
Winds met in conflict, each by turns supreme;
And, from the perilous ground dislodged, through storm
And rain he wildered on, no moon to stream
From gulf of parting clouds one friendly beam,
Nor any friendly sound his footsteps led;
Once did the lightning's faint disastrous gleam
Disclose a naked guide-post's double head,
Sight which, tho' lost at once, a gleam of pleasure shed.

from

"TIS SAID THAT SOME HAVE DIED FOR LOVE'

'Oh, move, thou Cottage, from behind that oak!
Or let the aged tree uprooted lie,
That in some other way yon smoke
May mount into the sky!
The clouds pass on; they from the heavens depart:
I look—the sky is empty space:
I know not what I trace;
But when I cease to look, my hand is on my heart.

'Oh! what a weight is in these shades! Ye leaves,
That murmur once so dear, when will it cease?
Your sound my heart of rest bereaves,
It robs my heart of peace.
Thou Thrush, that singest loud—and loud and free,
Into yon row of willows flit,
Upon that alder sit;
Or sing another song, or choose another tree.

'Roll back, sweet Rill! back to thy mountain-bounds,
And there for ever be thy waters chained!
For thou dost haunt the air with sounds
That cannot be sustained;
If still beneath that pine-tree's ragged bough
Headlong yon waterfall must come,
Oh let it then be dumb!
Be anything, sweet Rill, but that which thou art now.

'Thou Eglantine, so bright with sunny showers,
Proud as a rainbow spanning half the vale,
Thou one fair shrub, oh! shed thy flowers,
And stir not in the gale.
For thus to see thee nodding in the air,
To see thy arch thus stretch and bend,
Thus rise and thus descend—
Disturbs me till the sight is more than I can bear.'

from

THE WAGGONER

'Tis spent—this burning day of June!
Soft darkness o'er its latest gleams is stealing;
The buzzing dor-hawk, round and round, is wheeling,—
That solitary bird
Is all that can be heard
In silence deeper far than that of deepest noon!

Confiding Glow-worms, 'tis a night
Propitious to your earth-born light!
But where the scattered stars are seen
In hazy straits the clouds between,
Each, in his station twinkling not,
Seems changed into a pallid spot.
The mountains against heaven's grave weight
Rise up, and grow to wondrous height.
The air, as in a lion's den,
Is close and hot;—and now and then
Comes a tired and sultry breeze
With a haunting and a panting,
Like the stifling of disease;
But the dews allay the heat,
And the silence makes it sweet.

Hush, there is some one on the stir!
'Tis Benjamin the Waggoner;
Who long hath trod this toilsome way,
Companion of the night and day.
That far-off tinkling's drowsy cheer,
Mixed with a faint yet grating sound
In a moment lost and found,
The Wain announces—by whose side
Along the banks of Rydal Mere
He paces on, a trusty Guide,—
Listen! you can scarcely hear!
Hither he his course is bending;—

Now he leaves the lower ground,
And up the craggy hill ascending
Many a stop and stay he makes,
Many a breathing-fit he takes;
Steep the way and wearisome,
Yet all the while his whip is dumb!

WILLIAM WORDSWORTH 1770–1850

NUTTING

                              It seems a day
(I speak of one from many singled out)
One of those heavenly days that cannot die;
When, in the eagerness of boyish hope,
I left our cottage-threshold, sallying forth
With a huge wallet o'er my shoulders slung,
A nutting-crook in hand; and turned my steps
Tow'rd some far-distant wood, a Figure quaint,
Tricked out in proud disguise of cast-off weeds
Which for that service had been husbanded,
By exhortation of my frugal Dame—
Motley accoutrement, of power to smile
At thorns, and brakes, and brambles,—and in truth
More ragged than need was! O'er pathless rocks,
Through beds of matted fern, and tangled thickets,
Forcing my way, I came to one dear nook
Unvisited, where not a broken bough
Drooped with its withered leaves, ungracious sign
Of devastation; but the hazels rose
Tall and erect, with tempting clusters hung,
A virgin scene!—A little while, I stood,
Breathing with such suppression of the heart
As joy delights in; and with wise restraint
Voluptuous, fearless of a rival, eyed
The banquet;—or beneath the trees I sate
Among the flowers, and with the flowers I played;
A temper known to those who, after long
And weary expectation, have been blest
With sudden happiness beyond all hope.

Perhaps it was a bower beneath whose leaves
The violets of five seasons re-appear
And fade, unseen by any human eye;
Where fairy water-breaks do murmur on
For ever; and I saw the sparkling foam,
And—with my cheek on one of those green stones
That, fleeced with moss, under the shady trees,
Lay round me, scattered like a flock of sheep—
I heard the murmur and the murmuring sound,
In that sweet mood when pleasure loves to pay
Tribute to ease; and, of its joy secure,
The heart luxuriates with indifferent things,
Wasting its kindliness on stocks and stones,
And on the vacant air. Then up I rose,
And dragged to earth both branch and bough, with crash
And merciless ravage: and the shady nook
Of hazels, and the green and mossy bower,
Deformed and sullied, patiently gave up
Their quiet being: and unless I now
Confound my present feelings with the past,
Ere from the mutilated bower I turned
Exulting, rich beyond the wealth of kings,
I felt a sense of pain when I beheld
The silent trees, and saw the intruding sky.—
Then, dearest Maiden, move along these shades
In gentleness of heart; with gentle hand
Touch—for there is a spirit in the woods.

WILLIAM WORDSWORTH 1770–1850

WESTMINSTER BRIDGE

Earth has not anything to show more fair:
Dull would he be of soul who could pass by
A sight so touching in its majesty:
This city now doth, like a garment, wear
The beauty of the morning; silent, bare,
Ships, towers, domes, theatres, and temples lie
Open unto the fields, and to the sky;
All bright and glittering in the smokeless air.

Never did sun more beautifully steep
In his first splendour, valley, rock, or hill;
Ne'er saw I, never felt, a calm so deep!
The river glideth at his own sweet will:
Dear God! the very houses seem asleep;
And all that mighty heart is lying still!

WILLIAM WORDSWORTH 1770–1850

SONNET

There is a little unpretending Rill
Of limpid water, humbler far than aught
That ever among Men or Naiads sought
Notice or name!—It quivers down the hill,
Furrowing its shallow way with dubious will;
Yet to my mind this scanty stream is brought
Oftener than Ganges or the Nile; a thought
Of private recollection sweet and still!
Months perish with their moons; year treads on year;
But, faithful Emma! thou with me canst say
That, while ten thousand pleasures disappear,
And flies their memory fast almost as they;
The immortal Spirit of one happy day
Lingers beside that Rill, in vision clear.

WILLIAM WORDSWORTH 1770–1850

THE WILD DUCK'S NEST

The imperial Consort of the Fairy-king
Owns not a sylvan bower; or gorgeous cell
With emerald floored, and with purpureal shell
Ceilinged and roofed; that is so fair a thing
As this low structure, for the tasks of Spring
Prepared by one who loves the buoyant swell
Of the brisk waves, yet here consents to dwell;
And spreads in steadfast peace her brooding wing.
Words cannot paint the o'ershadowing yew-tree bough,
And dimly-gleaming Nest—a hollow crown

Of golden leaves inlaid with silver down,
Fine as the mother's softest plumes allow:
I gazed—and, self-accused while gazing, sighed
For human-kind, weak slaves of cumbrous pride!

WILLIAM WORDSWORTH 1770–1850

SONNET

How sweet it is, when mother Fancy rocks
The wayward brain, to saunter through a wood!
An old place, full of many a lovely brood,
Tall trees, green arbours, and ground-flowers in flocks;
And wild rose tip-toe upon hawthorn stocks,
Like a bold Girl, who plays her agile pranks
At Wakes and Fairs with wandering Mountebanks,—
When she stands cresting the Clown's head, and mocks
The crowd beneath her. Verily I think,
Such place to me is sometimes like a dream
Or map of the whole world: thoughts, link by link,
Enter through ears and eyesight, with such gleam
Of all things, that at last in fear I shrink,
And leap at once from the delicious stream.

WILLIAM WORDSWORTH 1770–1850

from

THE RIVER DUDDON

SONNET

V

Sole listener, Duddon! to the breeze that played
With thy clear voice, I caught the fitful sound
Wafted o'er sullen moss and craggy mound—
Unfruitful solitudes, that seemed to upbraid
The sun in heaven!—but now, to form a shade
For Thee, green alders have together wound
Their foliage; ashes flung their arms around;
And birch-trees risen in silver colonnade.
And thou hast also tempted here to rise,
'Mid sheltering pines, this Cottage rude and grey;

Rievaulx Abbey

Yorkshire

Whose ruddy children, by the mother's eyes
Carelessly watched, sport through the summer day,
Thy pleased associates:—light as endless May
On infant bosoms lonely Nature lies.

SAMUEL TAYLOR COLERIDGE 1772–1834
SONNET TO THE RIVER OTTER
Devon

Dear native Brook! wild Streamlet of the West!
　How many various-fated years have past,
　What happy and what mournful hours, since last
I skimmed the smooth thin stone along thy breast,
Numbering its light leaps! yet so deep imprest
Sink the sweet scenes of childhood, that mine eyes
　I never shut amid the sunny ray,
But straight with all their tints thy waters rise,
　Thy crossing plank, thy marge with willows grey,
And bedded sand that veined with various dyes
Gleamed through thy bright transparence! On my way
　Visions of Childhood! oft have ye beguiled
Lone manhood's cares, yet waking fondest sighs:
　Ah! that once more I were a careless Child!

SAMUEL TAYLOR COLERIDGE 1772–1834
from
FROST AT MIDNIGHT
Somerset

Therefore all seasons shall be sweet to thee,
Whether the summer clothe the general earth
With greenness, or the redbreast sit and sing
Betwixt the tufts of snow on the bare branch
Of mossy apple-tree, while the nigh thatch
Smokes in the sun-thaw; whether the eave-drops fall
Heard only in the trances of the blast,
Or if the secret ministry of frost
Shall hang them up in silent icicles,
Quietly shining to the quiet moon.

from

THE OLD MANSION

Cumberland

Old Man: Aye, master! fine old trees!
My grandfather could just remember back
When they were planted there. It was my task
To keep them trimm'd, and 'twas a pleasure to me:
All straight and smooth, and like a great green wall!
My poor old lady many a time would come
And tell me where to shear; for she had played
In childhood under them, and 'twas her pride
To keep them in their beauty. Plague, I say,
On their new-fangled whimsies! We shall have
A modern shrubbery here stuck full of firs
And your pert poplar trees. I could as soon
Have ploughed my father's grave as cut them down!

Stranger: But 'twill be lighter and more cheerful now—
A fine smooth turfe, and with a gravel road
Round for the carriage—now it suits my taste.
I like a shrubbery, too, it looks so fresh;
And then there's some variety about it.
In spring the lilac and the Gueldres rose,
And the laburnum with its golden flowers
Waving in the wind. And when the autumn comes,
The bright red berries of the mountain ash,
With firs enough in winter to look green,
And show that something lives. Sure this is better
Than a great hedge of yew that makes it look
All the year round like winter, and for ever
Dropping its poisonous leaves from the under boughs
So dry and bare!

Old Man: Ah! so the new squire thinks!

JOHN LEYDEN 1775–1811

from

SCENES OF INFANCY

Roxburghshire

Again, beside this silver rivulet's shore,
With green and yellow moss-flowers mottlied o'er,
Beneath a shivering canopy reclined,
Of aspen leaves, that wave without a wind,
I love to lie, when lulling breezes stir
The spiry cones that tremble on the fir,
Or wander mid the dark-green fields of broom,
When peers, in scattered tufts, the yellow bloom,
Or trace the path, with tangling furze o'er-run;
When bursting seed-bells crackle in the sun,
And pittering grasshoppers, confusedly shrill,
Pipe giddily along the glowing hill.
    Sweet grasshopper, who lovest at noon to lie
Serenely in the green-ribbed clover's eye,
To sun thy filmy wings, and emerald vest,
Unseen thy form, and undisturbed thy rest!

WALTER SAVAGE LANDOR 1775–1864

from

PROGRESS OF EVENING

Warwickshire

From yonder wood mark blue-eyed Eve proceed:
First thro' the deep and warm and secret glens,
Thro' the pale-glimmering privet-scented lane,
And thro' those alders by the river-side:
Now the soft dust impedes her, which the sheep
Have hollow'd out beneath their hawthorn shade.
But ah! look yonder! see a misty tide
Rise up the hill, lay low the frowning grove,
Enwrap the gay white mansion, sap its sides
Until they sink and melt away like chalk;

Now it comes down against our village-tower,
Covers its base, floats o'er its arches, tears
The clinging ivy from the battlements,
Mingles in broad embrace the obdurate stone,
(All one vast ocean), and goes swelling on
In slow and silent, dim and deepening waves.

WILLIAM STEWART ROSE 1775–1843

TO THE
RT. HON. JOHN HOOKHAM FRERE
IN MALTA

Sussex

Here, gladden'd by pure air and savour sweet
Of wild herb crush'd beneath my pony's feet,
I rove, when, warm'd by softer wind and shower,
They show their little blue or crimson flower.
Here, when the sun is low, and air is still,
And silence is upon the sea and hill,
Well-pleased I view the rampant lambs unite
To race, or match themselves in mimic fight,
Or through the prickly furze adventurous roam;
Till by the milky mothers summon'd home,
They quit their game, and ply their nimble feet,
In quick obedience to the peevish bleat.
    Here, oft descending through a double swell,
I dive into a little wooded dell,
Embosoming a hamlet, church and yard,
Whose graves, except some few of more regard
(Where wood a record of the dead preserves,
Or harder stone) are ridged with humble turves.
O'ergrown with greenwood is the curate's rest;
So screened, it might be called the parson's nest.
The chancel of the church in ochry stain
Shows Becket's death, before the altar slain:
And here, in red and yellow lines we trace,
As in Greek fictile vase, an odd, wild grace;
And in the knightly murderers' mail we read
The painter's toil coeval with the deed.

Merioneth

Trawsfynydd

from

MY NATIVE VILLAGE

Devon

Touched by the sunlight of the evening hour,
The elm still rises near thy aged tower
Dear, pensive Harewood, and in that rich ray
E'en thy old lichened battlements seem gay:—
Through the bowed windows streams the golden glow,
The beam is sleeping on the tombs below;
While, with its million flowers, yon hedge-row fair
Girts with green zone thy lowly House of Prayer.
No breezes play with amber leafage now,
Still is the cypress—still the ivy-bough,
And but for that fleet bird that glances round
Thy spire, or darting o'er the sacred ground
Twitters for very joy, how strange and deep
The silence where the lost—the loved ones sleep!

SIR CHARLES ABRAHAM ELTON 1778–1853

from

BOYHOOD

Somerset

   I stood upon a lawn whose greensward spread
Smooth-levell'd by the scythe; two mulberry trees
Beyond it stretch'd their old and foliaged arms;
Th' acacia quiver'd in the wind: the thick
And deep-leaved laurel darken'd the recess
Of massive buttresses; the mansion's walls,
Grey in antiquity, were tapestried o'er
With the fig's downy leaves, and roses climb'd
Clust'ring around the casements' gothic panes.
With terraces and verdant slopes, where pines
Arch'd their plumed boughs, and fruits espalier-train'd
Were mix'd with myrtles and with arbute-trees,

The scene behind look'd silvan: higher rose
The bounding hill, whose turfy paths were track'd
Up the bare herbage, gnarl'd with scatter'd crags
And topt with straggling firs or chestnuts broad;
A sweet yet solemn landscape, for it spoke
Of sacred home.

EBENEZER ELLIOTT 1781–1849

from

THE SPLENDID VILLAGE

Yorkshire

Path of the quiet fields! that oft of yore
Called me at morn, on Shenstone's page to pore:
O poor man's footpath! where at evening's close,
He stoop'd to pluck the woodbine and the rose,
Shaking the dewdrops from the wild-briar bowers,
That stoop'd beneath their load of summer flowers,
Then eyed the west, still bright with fading flame,
As whistling homeward by the wood he came;
Sweet, dewy, sunny, flowery footpath, thou
Art gone for ever, like the poor man's cow!
No more the wandering townsman's Sabbath smile—
No more the hedger waiting on the stile
For tardy Jane—no more the muttering bard,
Startling the heifer near the lone farm-yard—
No more the pious youth with book in hand,
Spelling the words he fain would understand,
Shall bless thy mazes, when the village bell
Sounds o'er the river, soften'd up the dell:
But from the parlour of the loyal inn,
The Great Unpaid, who cannot err nor sin,
Shall see, well-pleased, the pomp of Lawyer Ridge,
And poor Squire Grub's starved maids, and dandy bridge,
Where youngling fishers, in the grassy lane,
Purloined their tackle from the brood-mare's mane—
And truant urchins, by the river's brink,
Caught the fledged throstle as it stoop'd to drink—
Or with the ramping colt all joyous played,
Or scared the owlet in the bluebell'd shade.

64

from

SPIRITS AND MEN
Yorkshire

Again a child, where childhood rov'd, I run:
While groups of speedwell, with their bright blue eyes,
Like happy children, cluster in the sun.
Still the wan primrose hath a golden core;
The millefoil, thousand-leaf'd, as heretofore,
Displays a little world of flow'rets grey;
And tiny maids might hither come to cull
The woe-marked cowslip of the dewy May;
And still the fragrant thorn is beautiful.

EBENEZER ELLIOTT 1781–1849

WALKLEY

Sarah and William Adams! here we stood
   Roof'd by the cloud, which cast his frown between
Wardsend and Loxley's moorlands. From the wood
   Of one-starr'd Grenno, like a sea unseen,
The wind swept o'er us, seeming, in his might,
   To shake the steadfast rocks; while, rushing keen
Beyond the edge of darkness, stormy light,
   As from a league-wide trumpet, on the scene
A cataract of glory pour'd; and, bright
In gloom, the hill-tops islanded the night
   Of billowy shade around us. Vale and hill,
Forest and cloud, were restless as a fight;
   They seemed as they would never more be still;
While, anchor'd over all, the high-poised kite
Saw the foam'd rivers dash their blue with white.

from

ANSTER FAIR

Fifeshire

The saffron-elbow'd Morning up the slope
   Of heav'n canaries in her jewell'd shoes,
And throws o'er Kelly-law's sheep-nibbled top
   Her golden apron dripping kindly dews,
And never, since she first began to hop
   Up Heav'n's blue causeway, of her beams profuse,
Shone there a dawn so glorious and so gay,
As shines the merry dawn of ANSTER Market-day . . .

The fair Earth laughs through all her boundless range,
   Heaving her green hills high to greet the beam;
City and village, steeple, cot and grange,
   Gilt as with nature's purest leaf-gold seem;
The heaths and upland muirs, and fallows, change
   Their barren brown into a ruddy gleam,
And, on ten thousand dew-bent leaves and sprays,
Twinkle ten thousand suns and fling their petty rays.

Up from their nests and fields of tender corn
   Right merrily the little sky-larks spring,
And on their dew-bedabbled pinions born,
   Mount to the heav'n's blue key-stone flickering;
They turn their plume-soft bosoms to the morn,
   And hail the genial light and cheerly sing;
Echo the gladsome hills and valleys round,
And half the bells of Fife ring loud and swell the sound.

For, when the first up-sloping ray was flung
   On ANSTER steeple's swallow-harb'ring top,
It's bell and all the bells around were rung
   Sonorous, jangling loud without a stop,
For toilingly by each bitter beadle swung,
   Ev'n till he smok'd with sweat, his greasy rope,
And almost broke his bell-wheel, ush'ring in
The morn of ANSTER FAIR with tinkle-tankling din.

from

THE ANGLER'S TENT
Westmorland

How leapt our hearts, when from an airy height,
On which we passed for a sweet fountain's sake,
With green fields fading in a peaceful lake,
A deep-sunk vale burst sudden on our sight!
We felt as if at home; a magic sound,
As from a spirit whom we must obey,
Bade us descend into the vale profound,
And in its silence pass the Sabbath-day.
The placid lake that rested far below,
Softly embosoming another sky,
Still as we gazed assumed a lovelier glow,
And seemed to send us looks of amity.
Our hearts were open to the gracious love
Of Nature, smiling like a happy bride;
So following the hill's impulse from above,
Down the green slope we wind with airy glide,
And pitch our snowy tent on that fair water's side.

Ah me! even now I see before me stand,
Among the verdant holly-boughs half-hid,
The little radiant airy Pyramid,
Like some wild dwelling built in Fairy-land.
As silently as gathering cloud it rose,
And seemed a cloud descended on the earth,
Disturbing not the Sabbath-day's repose,
Yet gently stirring at the quiet birth
Of every short-lived breeze: the sunbeams greet
The beauteous stranger in the lonely bay;
Close to its shading tree two streamlets meet,
With gentle glide, as weary of their play.
And in the liquid lustre of the lake
Its image sleeps, reflected far below;
Such image as the clouds of summer make,
Clear seen amid the waveless water's glow,
As slumbering infant still, and pure as April snow.

from

THE BIRTHDAY

Hampshire

Say with a friend we contemplate some scene
Of natural loveliness, from which the heart
Drinks in its fill of deep admiring joy;
Some landscape scene, all glorious with the glow
Of summer evening, when the recent shower,
Transient and sudden, all the dry white road
Has moistened to red firmness; every leaf,
Washed from the dust, restored to glossy green;—
In such an evening oft the setting Sun,
Flaming in gold and purple clouds, comes forth
To take his farewell of our hemisphere;
Sudden the face of Nature brightens o'er
With such effulgence, as no painter's art
May imitate with faint similitude.
The rain-drops dripping fast from every spray
Are liquid topazes; bright emeralds those
Set on the green foil of the glistening leaves,
And every little hollow, concave stone,
And pebbly wheel-track, holds its sparkling pool
Brimming with molten amber. Of those drops
The Blackbird lights to drink; then scattering thick
A diamond shower among his dusty plumes,
Flies up rejoicing to some neighbouring elm,
And pours forth such a strain as wakens up
The music of unnumbered choristers.

CAROLINE BOWLES SOUTHEY 1786–1854

from

THE EVENING WALK

Hampshire

My lonely ramble yester-eve I took,
Along the pleasant path that by the brook,
Skirting its flowery margin, winds away
Through fields all fragrant now with new-mown hay.

I could not choose but linger as I went,
A willing idler, with a child's content,
Gathering the wildflowers on that streamlet's edge,
Spared by the mower's scythe, a fringing ledge.
Of spiky purple, epilobium tall,
Veronicas, and cuplike coronal
Of golden crowsfoot, waving meadow-sweet,
And wilding rose, that dipped the stream to meet.
And that small brook, so shallow and so clear!
The mother-ewe, without a mother's fear,
Led her young lamb from off the shelving brink,
Firm in the midway stream to stand and drink.
'Twas pleasant, as it dipped and gazed, to see
Its wonder at the watery mimicry,
As here and there, the ripple glancing by,
Imaged an up-drawn foot, a round black eye,
Wide staring, and a nose to meet its own
That seemed advancing from below.

WILLIAM HOLLOWAY fl. 1803

from
SCENES OF YOUTH
Dorset

Remember'd long, adown the far-stretch'd vale, . . .
Where elms, from Nature's hand confus'dly thrown,
With brushy trunks, in distance thick'ning, rise, . . .
The scattered hamlets interspers'd appear:
White are the cottage walls, save where the veil
Of dark-green ivy, rustling in the breeze,
Shivers along the eaves, where here and there
A flapping casement glitters, like the eyes
Of nubile maiden, from beneath the shade
Of sable gauze, that hides her blushing cheek
From 'saucy observation'. Soft and slow,
In mazes serpentine, a brimming rill
Visits the farm yard and the dairy door,
In front of which, a slab of oak or stone
Yields safe conveyance to the passing swain.

from

ON UVEDALE PRICE'S ESSAY

A master mind, that Taste and Genius grace,
The fine designs of Nature's hand can trace;
Where they may differ, where again we see
The beautiful and picturesque agree. . .
How sudden bursts of sunshine in the spring
O'er the green flourishing tree their lustre fling;
The delicate foliage of the leaf conceals
In part the boughs beneath, in part reveals.
How undulate the boughs in wavy pride,
As sweeps the light breeze o'er the river's tide:
How distant openings through the glade invite
Inquiry, source of ever new delight;
Leading the eye as in a wanton chase,
Onwards, with happy art *creating* space:
Itself the same through combinations new
Changes from every spot beheld the view,
Advances here a wood, and there recedes
A stream, again, far glittering o'er the meads!
How stretch along the hills, around, above,
Trees singly, or in groups, or lengthen'd grove.
How fan-like branches of the cedar, spread
Magnificently, feather overhead,
In avenues, of which the pillar'd shade
Attracts the devotee, or love-sick maid.
How on its gorgeous canopy of leaves
The widely-branching chestnut light receives.

Approach to Gordale Scar

Yorkshire

A SUMMER EVENING CHURCHYARD
LECHLADE

Gloucestershire

The wind has swept from the wide atmosphere
Each vapour that obscured the sunset's ray;
And pallid Evening twines its beaming hair
In duskier braids around the languid eyes of Day:
Silence and Twilight, unbeloved of men,
Creep hand in hand from yon obscurest glen.

They breathe their spells towards the departing day,
Encompassing the earth, air, stars, and sea;
Light, sound, and motion own the potent sway,
Responding to the charm with its own mystery.
The winds are still, or the dry church-tower grass
Knows not their gentle motions as they pass.

Thou too, aëreal Pile! whose pinnacles
Point from one shrine like pyramids of fire,
Obeyest in silence their sweet solemn spells,
Clothing in hues of heaven thy dim and distant spire,
Around whose lessening and invisible height
Gather among the stars the clouds of night.

The dead are sleeping in their sepulchres:
And, mouldering as they sleep, a thrilling sound,
Half sense, half thought, among the darkness stirs,
Breathed from their wormy beds all living things around,
And mingling with the still night and mute sky
Its awful hush is felt inaudibly.

Thus solemnized and softened, death is mild
And terrorless as this serenest night:
Here could I hope, like some inquiring child
Sporting on graves, that death did hide from human sight
Sweet secrets, or beside its breathless sleep
That loveliest dreams perpetual watch did keep.

71

WALK TO CHURCH

The path of the Just is as the shining light, that shineth more and more unto the perfect day.—Proverbs iv, 18.

Now the holy hour is nigh,
  Seek we out the holy ground;
Overhead the breezy sky,
  Rustling woodlands all around:
Fragrant streams from oak-leaves sere,
  Peat and moss and whortles green,
Dews that yet are glistening clear
  Through their brown or briery screen.

Hie we through the autumnal wood,
  Pausing where the echoes dwell,
Boys, or men of boyish mood,
  Trying how afar they swell.
Haply down some opening glade
  Now the old grey tower we see,
Underneath whose solemn shade
  Jesus risen hath sworn to be.

He hath sworn, for there will meet
  Two or three in His great name,
Waiting till their incense sweet
  Feel His heaven-descended flame.
Day by day that old grey tower
  Tells its tale, and week by week
In their tranquil hoary bower
  To the unlearned its shadows speak.

THE OAK

*What went ye out into the wilderness to see? A reed shaken with
the wind?*—St. Matthew xi, 7.

Come take a woodland walk with me,
And mark the rugged old Oak Tree,
How steadily his arm he flings
Where from the bank the fresh rill springs,
And points the waters' silent way
Down the wild maze of reed and spray.
Two furlongs on they glide unseen,
Known only by the livelier green.

There stands he, in each time and tide,
The new-born streamlet's guard and guide.
To him spring shower and summer sun,
Brown autumn, winter's sleet, are one.
But firmest in the bleakest hour
He holds his root in faith and power,
The splinter'd bark, his girdle stern,
His robe, grey moss and mountain fern.

Mark'st thou in him no token true
Of heaven's own Priests, both old and new,
In penitential garb austere
Fix'd in the wild, from year to year
The lessons of stern love to teach,
To penitents and children preach,
Bold words and eager glances stay,
And gently level Jesus' way?

ON A LANE IN SPRING

Northamptonshire

A little lane—the brook runs close beside,
  And spangles in the sunshine, while the fish glide swiftly by;
And hedges leafing with the green springtide;
  From out their greenery the old birds fly,
And chirp and whistle in the morning sun;
  The pilewort glitters 'neath the pale blue sky,
The little robin has its nest begun,
  The grass-green linnets round the bushes fly.
How mild the spring comes in! the daisy buds
  Lift up their golden blossoms to the sky.
How lovely are the pingles in the woods!
  Here a beetle runs—and there a fly
Rests on the arum leaf in bottle-green,
And all the spring in this sweet lane is seen.

JOHN CLARE 1793-1864

YOUNG JENNY

Northamptonshire

The cockchafer hums down the rut-rifted lane
Where the wild roses hang and the woodbines entwine,
And the shrill squeaking bat makes his circles again
Round the side of the tavern close by the sign.
The sun is gone down like a wearisome queen,
In curtains the richest that ever were seen.

The dew falls on flowers in a mist of small rain,
And, beating the hedges, low fly the barn-owls;
The moon with her horns is just peeping again,
And deep in the forest the dog-badger howls;
In best bib and tucker then wanders my Jane
By the side of the woodbines which grow in the lane.

Easegill   *Lancashire*

On a sweet eventide I walk by her side;
In green hoods the daisies have shut up their eyes.
Young Jenny is handsome without any pride;
Her eyes (oh, how bright!) have the hue of the skies.
Oh, 'tis pleasant to walk by the side of my Jane
At the close of the day, down the mossy green lane.

We stand by the brook, by the gate, and the stile,
While the even star hangs out his lamp in the sky;
And on her calm face dwells a sweet sunny smile,
While her soul fondly speaks through the light of her eye.
Sweet are the moments while waiting for Jane;
'Tis her footsteps I hear coming down the green lane.

JOHN CLARE 1793–1864

AUTUMN

Northamptonshire

I love the fitful gust that shakes
   The casement all the day,
And from the mossy elm tree takes
   The faded leaves away,
Twirling them by the window pane
With thousand others down the lane.

I love to see the shaking twig
   Dance till the shut of eve,
The sparrow on the cottage rig,
   Whose chirp would make believe
That spring was just now flirting by
In summer's lap with flowers to lie.

I love to see the cottage smoke
   Curl upwards through the trees,
The pigeons nestled round the cote
   On November days like these;
The cock upon the dunghill crowing,
The mill-sails on the heath a-going.

The feather from the raven's breast
   Falls on the stubble lea;
The acorns near the old crow's nest
   Drop pattering down the tree;
The grunting pigs, that wait for all,
Scramble and hurry where they fall.

FELICIA DOROTHEA HEMANS 1794–1835

SABBATH SONNET

How many blessèd groups this hour are bending,
   Through England's primrose meadow-paths, their way
Towards spire and tower, 'midst shadowy elms ascending,
   Whence the sweet chimes proclaim the hallowed day!
   The halls from old heroic ages grey
Pour their fair children forth; and hamlets low,
   With whose thick orchard-blooms the soft winds play,
Send out their inmates in a happy flow,
Like a freed vernal stream. I may not tread
With them those pathways—to the feverish bed
   Of sickness bound; yet, O my God! I bless
Thy mercy, that with Sabbath-peace hath filled
My chastened heart, and all its throbbing stilled
   To one deep calm of lowliest thankfulness!

ROBERT POLLOK 1798–1827

from

THE COURSE OF TIME
Renfrewshire

Much of my native scenery appears,
And presses forward to be in my song;
But must not now, for much behind awaits
Of higher note. Four trees I pass not by,
Which o'er our house their evening shadow threw,
Three ash, and one of elm. Tall trees they were,
And old, and had been old a century
Before my day. None living could say aught

About their youth; but they were goodly trees:
And oft I wondered, as I sat and thought
Beneath their summer shade, or, in the night
Of winter, heard the spirits of the wind
Howling among their boughs,—how they had grown
So high, in such a rough tempestuous place;
And when a hapless branch, torn by the blast,
Fell down, I mourned as if a friend had fallen.

DAVID MOIR 1798–1851

from

THE ANGLER

Midlothian

Early a-foot,
On public roads, and by each hedge-way path,
From the far North, and from Hibernia's strand,
With vestures many-hued, and ceaseless chat,
The reapers to the coming harvest plied—
Father and mother, stripling, and young child
On back or shoulder borne. I trod again
A scene of youth, bright in its natural lines
Even to a stranger's eyes when first time seen,
But sanctified to mine by many a fond
And faithful recognition. O'er the Esk,
Swoln by nocturnal showers, the hawthorn hung
Its garland of green berries, and the bramble
Trail'd 'mid the camomile its ripening fruit.
Most lovely was the verdure of the hills—
A rich, luxuriant green, o'er which the sky
Of blue, translucent, clear without a cloud,
Outspread its arching amplitude serene.
With many a gush of music, from each brake
Sang forth the choral linnets; and the lark,
Ascending from the clover field, by fits
Soared as it sang, and dwindled from the sight.
The cushat stood amidst the topmost boughs
Of the tall tree, his white-ring'd neck aslant,

Down thro' the leaves to see his brooding mate.
'Mid the tall meadow-grass the ox reclined,
Or bent his knee, or from beneath the shade
Of the broad beech, with ruminant mouth, gaz'd forth.
Rustling with wealth, a tissue of fair fields
Outstretch'd to left and right in luxury;
And the fir forests on the upland slopes
Contrasted darkly with the golden grain.

REV. WILLIAM BARNES 1801-1886

HILL AND DELL

Dorset

At John's, up at Sandhills, 'tis healthy and dry,
Though I may not like it, it may be—not I.
Where fir-trees are spindling, with tapering tops,
From leafy-leav'd fern in the cold stunted copse,
And under keen gorsebrakes, all yellow in bloom,
The skylark's brown nest is deep-hidden in gloom;
And high on the cliff, where no foot ever wore
A path to the threshold, 's the sandmartin's door,
On waterless heights, while the winds lowly sigh,
On tree-climbing ivy, before the blue sky.

I think I could hardly like his place as well
As my own shelter'd home in the timbery dell,
When rooks come to build in the high-swaying boughs,
And broadheaded oaks yield a shade for the cows;
Where grey-headed withy-trees lean o'er the brook
Of grey-lighted waters that whirl by the nook,
And only the girls and the swans are in white,
Like snow on grey moss in the midwinter's light,
And wind softly drives, with a low rustling sound,
By waves on the water and grass on the ground.

SHEEP IN THE SHADE

Dorset

In summer time, I took my road
From stile to stile, from ground to ground,
The while the cloudless sunshine glowed,
On down and mead, by sun-heat browned,
Where slowly round a wide-bent bow
The stream wound on, with water low:
In hopeful hours that glided on,
With me in happiness now gone.

And there, below the elm-tree shroud,
Where shaded air might cooler swim,
There lay a quickly-panting crowd
Of sheep, within the shadow's rim,
That glided slowly, on and on,
Till there they lay, with shadow gone.
And oh! that happy hours should glide
Away so soon, with time and tide.

SHELLBROOK

Dorset

When out by Shellbrook, round by stile and tree,
With longer days and sunny hours come on,
With spring and all its sunny showers come on,
With May and all its shining flowers come on,
How merry, young with young would meet in glee.

And there, how we in merry talk went by
The foam below the river bay, all white,
The blossom on the green-leav'd may, all white,
And chalk beside the dusty way, all white,
Where glitt'ring water match'd with blue the sky.

Or else in winding paths and lanes, along
The timb'ry hillocks, sloping steep, we roam'd;
Or down the dells and dingles deep we roam'd;
Or by the bending brook's wide sweep we roam'd
On holidays, with merry laugh or song.

But now, the frozen churchyard wallings keep
The patch of tower-shaded ground, all white,
Where friends can find the frosted mound, all white
With turfy sides upswelling round, all white
With young offsunder'd from the young in sleep.

THOMAS AIRD 1802–1876

from

FRANK SYLVAN

Roxburghshire

O! now the summer woods! and O! the joy
To haunt their tangled depths, with curious eye
Watching the wild folk of the leafy world,
From beetledom below to the high flight
Of shooting doves that shave the liquid air!
Such pastime has been Frank's, since first, a boy,
When lit the rising sun with level rays
The light green glimmering of the barley braird,
Empearled with dew, till all the trembling drops
Like sapphires glowed, he wondered at the hare
Hirpling therein, and sitting oft on end
With strange suspicious murgeons—can it be
Old Eppie Tait, the witch? and wondering saw
The horse-hair stirring in the shallow pool,
Left in the rut of the unmended road,
After warm rains by night—will it become
A lamprey, as they say? and wondering found
The shrew-mouse lying, with its entrails out,
On the green path, where late at eve he passed
And saw it not—what killed it? was't the owl
By night who pounced it for a common mouse,
And, out of temper at her own mistake,
Tore it to death, but scorned to taste a shrew?

A RAPTURE ON THE CORNISH HILLS

I stood at the foot of Rocky Carradon—
The massive monuments of a vast religion,
Piled by the strength of unknown hands, were there.
The everlasting hills, around, afar,
Uplifted their huge fronts, the natural altars
Reared by the Earth to its surrounding God.
I heard a Voice, as the sound of many waters:—
'What do'st thou here, Elijah?' And I said,
'What doth *he* here, Man that is born of woman?
The clouds may haunt these mountains; the fierce storm
Coiled in his caverned lair—that wild torrent
Leaps from a native land: but Man! O Lord!
What doth *he* here!'
Stranger: Did'st thou not fear the Voice?
The Bard: I could not, at the foot of Rocky Carradon.

from

THE QUEST OF THE SANGRAAL
Cornwall

There the brown barrow curves its sullen breast,
Above the bones of some dead Gentile's soul:
All husht—and calm—and cold—until anon
Gleams the old dawn—the well-remembered day—
Then may you hear, beneath that hollow cairn,
The clash of arms: the muffled shout of war;
Blent with the rustle of the kindling dead!

from

AURORA LEIGH

Herefordshire

I dared to rest, or wander,—like a rest
Made sweeter for the step upon the grass,—
And view the ground's most gentle dimplement,
(As if God's finger touched but did not press
In making England!) such an up and down
Of verdure,—nothing too much up or down,
A ripple of land; such little hills, the sky
Can stoop to tenderly and the wheatfields climb;
Such nooks of valleys, lined with orchises,
Fed full of noises by invisible streams;
And open pastures, where you scarcely tell
White daisies from white dew,—at intervals
The mythic oaks and elm-trees standing out
Self-poised upon their prodigy of shade,—
I thought my father's land was worthy too
Of being my Shakespeare's . . .
                         Then the thrushes sang,
And shook my pulses and the elms' new leaves . . .
I flattered all the beauteous country round,
As poets use; the skies, the clouds, the fields,
The happy violets hiding from the roads
The primroses run down to, carrying gold,—
The tangled hedgerows, where the cows push out
Impatient horns and tolerant churning mouths
'Twixt dripping ash-boughs,—hedgerows all alive
With birds and gnats and large white butterflies
Which look as if the May-flower had caught life
And palpitated forth upon the wind,—
Hills, vales, woods, netted in a silver mist,
Farm, granges, doubled up among the hills,
And cattle grazing in the watered vales,
And cottage-chimneys smoking from the woods,
And cottage-gardens smelling everywhere,
Confused with smell of orchards.

THE CHARMING OF THE EAST WIND

Lincolnshire

Late in the month a rough east wind had sway,
The old trees thunder'd, and the dust was blown;
But other powers possess'd the night and day,
And soon he found he could not hold his own;
The merry ruddock whistled at his heart,
And strenuous blackbirds pierced his flanks with song,
Pert sparrows wrangled o'er his every part,
And through him shot the larks on pinions strong:
Anon a sunbeam broke across the plain,
And the wild bee went forth on booming wing—
Whereat he feeble wax'd, but rose again
With aimless rage, and idle blustering;
The south wind touch'd him with a drift of rain,
And down he sank, a captive to the spring!

A BRILLIANT DAY

Lincolnshire

O keen pellucid air! nothing can lurk
Or disavow itself on this bright day;
The small rain-plashes shine from far away,
The tiny emmet glitters at his work;
The bee looks blithe and gay, and as she plies
Her task, and moves and sidles round the cup
Of this spring flower, to drink its honey up,
Her glassy wings, like oars that dip and rise,
Gleam momently. Pure-bosom'd, clear of fog,
The long lake glistens, while the glorious beam
Bespangles the wet joints and floating leaves
Of water-plants, whose every point receives
His light; and jellies of the spawning frog,
Unmark'd before, like piles of jewels seem!

THE HOME FIELD. EVENING

Lincolnshire

'Tis sweet, when slanting light the field adorns,
To see the new-shorn flocks recline or browse;
While swallows flit among the restful cows,
Their gurgling dew-laps, and their harmless horns;
Or flirt the aged hunter, in his dose,
With passing wing; yet with no thought to grieve
His mild, unjealous, innocent repose,
With those keen contrasts our sad hearts conceive.
And then, perchance, the evening wind awakes
With sudden tumult, and the bowery ash
Goes storming o'er the golden moon, whose flash
Fills and refills its breezy gaps and breaks;
The weeping willow at her neighbour floats,
And busy rustlings stir the wheat and oats.

ALFRED LORD TENNYSON 1809–1892

from

THE GARDENER'S DAUGHTER

Lightly he laugh'd, as one that read my thought,
And on we went; but ere an hour had pass'd,
We reach'd a meadow slanting to the North;
Down which a well-worn pathway courted us
To one green wicket in a privet hedge;
This, yielding, gave into a grassy walk
Thro' crowded lilac-ambush trimly pruned;
And one warm gust, full-fed with perfume, blew
Beyond us, as we enter'd in the cool.
The garden stretches southward. In the midst
A cedar spread his dark-green layers of shade.
The garden-glasses glanced, and momently
The twinkling laurel scatter'd silver lights.

'Eustace,' I said, 'this wonder keeps the house.'
He nodded, but a moment afterwards
He cried, 'Look! look!' Before he ceased I turn'd,
And, ere a star can wink, beheld her there.

For up the porch there grew an Eastern rose,
That, flowering high, the last night's gale had caught,
And blown across the walk. One arm aloft—
Gown'd in pure white, that fitted to the shape—
Holding the bush, to fix it back, she stood,
A single stream of all her soft brown hair
Pour'd on one side: the shadow of the flowers
Stole all the golden gloss, and, wavering
Lovingly lower, trembled on her waist—
Ah, happy shade—and still went wavering down,
But, ere it touch'd a foot, that might have danced
The greensward into greener circles, dipt,
And mix'd with shadows of the common ground!

ALFRED LORD TENNYSON 1809–1892

from

THE PRINCESS

'Come out,' he said,
'To the Abbey: there is Aunt Elizabeth
And sister Lilia with the rest.' We went
(I kept the book and had my finger in it)
Down thro' the park: strange was the sight to me;
For all the sloping pasture murmur'd, sown
With happy faces and with holiday.
There moved the multitude, a thousand heads:
The patient leaders of their Institute
Taught them with facts. One rear'd a font of stone
And drew, from butts of water on the slope,
The fountain of the moment, playing, now
A twisted snake, and now a rain of pearls,
Or steep-up spout whereon the gilded ball
Danced like a wisp: and somewhat lower down
A man with knobs and wires and vials fired
A cannon: Echo answer'd in her sleep
From hollow fields: and here were telescopes

For azure views; and there a group of girls
In circle waited, whom the electric shock
Dislink'd with shrieks and laughter: round the lake
A little clock-work steamer paddling plied
And shook the lilies: perch'd about the knolls
A dozen angry models jetted steam:
A petty railway ran: a fire-balloon
Rose gem-like up before the dusky groves
And dropt a fairy parachute and past:
And there thro' twenty posts of telegraph
They flash'd a saucy message to and fro
Between the mimic stations; so that sport
Went hand in hand with Science; otherwhere
Pure sport: a herd of boys with clamour bowl'd
And stump'd the wicket; babies roll'd about
Like tumbled fruit in grass; and men and maids
Arranged a country dance, and flew thro' light
And shadow, while the twangling violin
Struck up with Soldier-laddie, and overhead
The broad ambrosial aisles of lofty lime
Made noise with bees and breeze from end to end.
    Strange was the sight and smacking of the time;
And long we gazed, but satiated at length
Came to the ruins. High-arch'd and ivy-claspt,
Of finest Gothic lighter than a fire,
Thro' one wide chasm of time and frost they gave
The park, the crowd, the house; but all within
The sward was trim as any garden lawn: ·
And here we lit on Aunt Elizabeth,
And Lilia with the rest, and lady friends
From neighbour seats: and there was Ralph himself,
A broken statué propt against the wall,
As gay as any. Lilia, wild with sport,
Half child half woman as she was, had wound
A scarf of orange round the stony helm,
And robed the shoulders in a rosy silk,
That made the old warrior from his ivied nook
Glow like a sunbeam: near his tomb a feast
Shone, silver-set; about it lay the guests,
And there we join'd them.

from

THE BROOK

'O Katie, what I suffer'd for your sake!
For in I went, and call'd old Philip out
To show the farm: full willingly he rose:
He led me thro' the short sweet-smelling lanes
Of his wheat-suburb, babbling as he went.
He praised his land, his horses, his machines;
He praised his ploughs, his cows, his hogs, his dogs;
He praised his hens, his geese, his guinea-hens;
His pigeons, who in session on their roofs
Approved him, bowing at their own deserts:
Then from the plaintive mother's teat he took
Her blind and shuddering puppies, naming each,
And naming those, his friends, for whom they were:
Then crost the common into Darnley chase
To show Sir Arthur's deer. In copse and fern
Twinkled the innumerable ear and tail.
Then, seated on a serpent-rooted beech,
He pointed out a pasturing colt, and said:
'That was the four-year-old I sold the Squire.'
And there he told a long long-winded tale
Of how the Squire had seen the colt at grass,
And how it was the thing his daughter wish'd,
And how he sent the bailiff to the farm
To learn the price, and what the price he ask'd,
And how the bailiff swore that he was mad,
But he stood firm; and so the matter hung;
He gave them line; and five days after that
He met the bailiff at the Golden Fleece,
Who then and there had offer'd something more,
But he stood firm; and so the matter hung;
He knew the man; the colt would fetch its price;
He gave them line: and how by chance at last
(It might be May or April, he forgot,
The last of April or the first of May)
He found the bailiff riding by the farm,
And, talking from the point, he drew him in,

And there he mellow'd all his heart with ale,
Until they closed a bargain, hand in hand.
  'Then, while I breathed in sight of haven, he,
Poor fellow, could he help it? recommenced,
And ran thro' all the coltish chronicle,
Wild Will, Black Bess, Tantivy, Tallyho,
Reform, White Rose, Bellerophon, the Jilt,
Arbaces, and Phenomenon, and the rest,
Till, not to die a listener, I arose
And with me Philip, talking still; and so
We turn'd our foreheads from the falling sun,
And following our own shadows thrice as long
As when they follow'd us from Philip's door,
Arrived and found the sun of sweet content
Re-risen in Katie's eyes, and all things well.'

ALFRED LORD TENNYSON 1809–1892

from

AYLMER'S FIELD

  A whisper half reveal'd her to herself.
For out beyond her lodges, where the brook
Vocal, with here and there a silence, ran
By sallowy rims, arose the labourers' homes,
A frequent haunt of Edith, on low knolls
That dimpling died into each other, huts
At random scatter'd, each a nest in bloom.
Her art, her hand, her counsel, all had wrought
About them: here was one that, summer-blanch'd,
Was parcel-bearded with the traveller's-joy
In Autumn, parcel ivy-clad; and here
The warm-blue breathings of a hidden hearth
Broke from a bower of vine and honeysuckle:
One look'd all rosetree, and another wore
A close-set robe of jasmine sown with stars:
This had a rosy sea of gillyflowers
About it; this, a milky-way on earth,
Like visions in the Northern dreamer's heavens,
A lily-avenue climbing to the doors;
One, almost to the martin-haunted eaves

A summer burial deep in hollyhocks;
Each, its own charm; and Edith's everywhere. . .

Then the great Hall was wholly broken down,
And the broad woodland parcell'd into farms;
And where the two contrived their daughter's good,
Lies the hawk's cast, the mole has made his run,
The hedgehog underneath the plantain bores,
The rabbit fondles his own harmless face,
The slow-worm creeps, and the thin weasel there
Follows the mouse, and all is open field.

ALFRED LORD TENNYSON 1809–1892

from

IN MEMORIAM

XI

Calm is the morn without a sound,
  Calm as to suit a calmer grief,
  And only thro' the faded leaf
The chestnut pattering to the ground:

Calm and deep peace on this high wold,
  And on these dews that drench the furze,
  And all the silvery gossamers
That twinkle into green and gold:

Calm and still light on yon great plain
  That sweeps with all its autumn bowers,
  And crowded farms and lessening towers,
To mingle with the bounding main:

Calm and deep peace in this wide air,
  These leaves that redden to the fall;
  And in my heart, if calm at all,
If any calm, a calm despair:

Calm on the seas, and silver sleep,
  And waves that sway themselves in rest,
  And dead calm in that noble breast
Which heaves but with the heaving deep.

To-night the winds begin to rise
   And roar from yonder dropping day:
   The last red leaf is whirl'd away,
The rooks are blown about the skies;

The forest crack'd, the waters curl'd,
   The cattle huddled on the lea;
   And wildly dash'd on tower and tree
The sunbeam strikes along the world:

And but for fancies, which aver
   That all thy motions gently pass
   Athwart a plane of molten glass,
I scarce could brook the strain and stir

That makes the barren branches loud;
   And but for fear it is not so,
   The wild unrest that lives in woe
Would dote and pore on yonder cloud

That rises upward always higher,
   And onward drags a labouring breast,
   And topples round the dreary west,
A looming bastion fringed with fire.

LXXXVII

I past beside the reverend walls
   In which of old I wore the gown;
   I roved at random thro' the town,
And saw the tumult of the halls;

And heard once more in college fanes
   The storm their high-built organs make,
   And thunder-music, rolling, shake
The prophet blazon'd on the panes;

And caught once more the distant shout,
   The measured pulse of racing oars
   Among the willows; paced the shores
And many a bridge, and all about

Berkshire

Park Place

The same gray flats again, and felt
   The same, but not the same; and last
   Up that long walk of limes I past
To see the rooms in which he dwelt. . .

XCV

By night we linger'd on the lawn,
   For underfoot the herb was dry;
   And genial warmth; and o'er the sky
The silvery haze of summer drawn;

And calm that let the tapers burn
   Unwavering: not a cricket chirr'd:
   The brook alone far-off was heard,
And on the board the fluttering urn:

And bats went round in fragrant skies,
   And wheel'd or lit the filmy shapes
   That haunt the dusk, with ermine capes
And woolly breasts and beaded eyes . . .

Till now the doubtful dusk reveal'd
   The knolls once more where, couch'd at ease,
   The white kine glimmer'd and the trees
Laid their dark arms about the field:

And suck'd from out the distant gloom
   A breeze began to tremble o'er
   The large leaves of the sycamore,
And fluctuate all the still perfume,

And gathering freshlier overhead,
   Rock'd the full-foliaged elms, and swung
   The heavy-folded rose, and flung
The lilies to and fro, and said

'The dawn, the dawn', and died away;
   And East and West, without a breath,
   Mixt their dim lights, like life and death,
To broaden into boundless day.

Unwatch'd, the garden bough shall sway,
　　The tender blossom flutter down,
　　Unloved, that beech will gather brown,
This maple burn itself away;

Unlov'd, the sun-flower, shining fair,
　　Ray round with flames her disk of seed,
　　And many a rose-carnation feed
With summer spice the humming air;

Unloved, by many a sandy bar,
　　The brook shall babble down the plain,
　　At noon or when the lesser wain
Is twisting round the polar star;

Uncared for, gird the windy grove,
　　And flood the haunts of hern and crake;
　　Or into silver arrows break
The sailing moon in creek and cove;

Till from the garden and the wild
　　A fresh association blow,
　　And year by year the landscape grow
Familiar to the stranger's child;

As year by year the labourer tills
　　His wonted glebe, or lops the glades;
　　And year by year our memory fades
From all the circle of the hills.

ALFRED LORD TENNYSON 1809–1892

from

THE PROGRESS OF SPRING

The groundflame of the crocus breaks the mould,
　Fair Spring slides hither o'er the Southern sea,
Wavers on her thin stem the snowdrop cold
　That trembles not to kisses of the bee:
Come, Spring, for now from all the dripping eaves
　The spear of ice has wept itself away,

And hour by hour unfolding woodbine leaves
  O'er his uncertain shadow droops the day.
She comes! The loosen'd rivulets run;
  The frost-bead melts upon her golden hair;
Her mantle, slowly greening in the sun,
  Now wraps her close, now arching leaves her bare,
  To breaths of balmier air;

Up leaps the lark, gone wild to welcome her,
  About her glance the tits, and shriek the jays,
Before her skims the jubilant woodpecker,
  The linnet's bosom blushes at her gaze,
While round her brows a woodland culver flits,
  Watching her large light eyes and gracious looks,
And in her open palm a halcyon sits
  Patient—the secret splendour of the brooks.
Come, Spring! She comes on waste and wood,
  On farm and field: but enter also here,
Diffuse thyself at will thro' all my blood,
  And, tho' thy violet sicken into sere,
  Lodge with me all the year!

Once more a downy drift against the brakes,
  Self-darken'd in the sky, descending slow!
But gladly see I thro' the wavering flakes
  Yon blanching apricot like snow in snow.
These will thine eyes not brook in forest-paths,
  On their perpetual pine, nor round the beech;
They fuse themselves to little spicy baths,
  Solved in the tender blushes of the peach;
They lose themselves and die
  On that new life that gems the hawthorn line;
Thy gay lent-lilies wave and put them by,
  And out once more in varnish'd glory shine
  Thy stars of celandine.

She floats across the hamlet. Heaven lours,
  But in the tearful splendour of her smiles
I see the slowly-thickening chestnut towers
  Fill out the spaces by the barren tiles.

Now past her feet the swallow circling flies,
    A clamorous cuckoo stoops to meet her hand;
Her light makes rainbows in my closing eyes,
    I hear a charm of song thro' all the land.
Come, Spring! She comes, and Earth is glad
    To roll her North below thy deepening dome,
But ere thy maiden birk be wholly clad,
        And these low bushes dip their twigs in foam,
        Make all true hearths thy home.

Across my garden! and the thicket stirs,
    The fountain pulses high in sunnier jets,
The blackcap warbles, and the turtle purrs,
    The starling claps his tiny castanets.
Still round her forehead wheels the woodland dove,
    And scatters on her throat the sparks of dew,
The kingcup fills her footprint, and above
    Broaden the glowing isles of vernal blue.
Hail ample presence of a Queen,
    Bountiful, beautiful, apparell'd gay,
Whose mantle, every shade of glancing green,
        Flies back in fragrant breezes to display
        A tunic white as May!

THOMAS FRANCIS fl. 1859

from

THE OFFSPRING

Pembrokeshire

Hard on the high road side, midway between
Haverfordwest and the industrious town
Of Fishguard, lies a vale. Narrow it is,
And picturesque. On either sloping side
Rocks recline, mellow with the weather's wear,
Rude broken, craggy and in heaps confused,
As if the earth, in time, now out of date,
Had, in this place, sustained eruptions wild.

Talland Church

Cornwall

Eastward there heaves a precipice sublime,
Terribly steep, o'ergrown with mountain heath,
And intersected, herbless to the sod,
With many a path, trod by the intrepid sheep,
Which nibbling here, sideways are ever seen.
Within the valley sounds the Cleddaw's song,
A dear old stream, along whose noisy banks
Often I've strayed, to store my bag with nuts,
Sorrowless as the winds that met my brow.

REV. HENRY ALFORD 1810–1871

THE MENDIP HILLS OVER WELLS
Somerset

How grand beneath the feet that company
    Of steep gray roofs and clustering pinnacles
Of the massy fane, brooding in majesty
    Above the town that spreads among the dells!
Hark! the deep clock unrolls its voice of power;
    And sweetly-mellowed sound of chiming bells
Calling to prayer from out the central tower
    Over the thickly-timbered hollow dwells.
Meet worship-place for such a glorious stretch
    Of sunny prospect—for these mighty hills,
And that dark solemn Tor, and all that reach
    Of bright-green meadows, laced with silver rills,
Bounded by ranges of pale blue, that rise
To where white strips of sea are traced upon the skies.

REV. F. W. FABER 1814–1863

ENNERDALE
Cumberland

    I thought of Ennerdale as of a thing
Upon the confines of my memory.
There was a hazy gleam as o'er a sheet
Of sunny water cast, and mountain side,

95

And much ploughed land, and cleanly cottages,
A bubbling brook, the emptying of the lake,
An indistinct remembrance of being pleased
That there were hedgerows there instead of walls,
That it was noon, and that I swam for long
In the warm lake, and dressed upon a rock :
And this is all of verdant Ennerdale
Which I can now recover from my mind;
The current of bright years hath washed it out.
    Yet do I find the memory of it still
A thing which I can lean upon, a spot
Of greenness and fresh water in my soul.
And I do feel the very knowledge good
That there is such a place as Ennerdale,
A valley and a lake of such a kind,
As though I did possess it all myself
With daily eye and ear, because I know
It is possessed by simple dalesmen there.
    And I have many Ennerdales, am rich
In woods and fields the owners think are theirs.
I can dispark the trim enclosures first,
And, in the very wantonness of power,
Forthwith enclose the black unfettered heath.
I pass along the road, and set my seal
On lawns, rough banks, wet coverts of wild flowers,
And I can pick out trees from forest lands,
For beauty or uncouthness singular,
As heriots; nay, the very brooks salute
Their master as they leap, tinkling to him,
Shrewd vassals! as their truest feudal lord,
With music such as they have never paid
Unto the self-called owner: when I walk
By night among the moistened woods they send
From every glen their dues of mossy smells,
And fragrance of the withered things which lie
Upon the woodland floor.
                                        I make a stir
Among the fields and flowery clods, as though
I would have something changed; I fold my arms,
And look around, and draw my breath; I gaze

Upon the fair estates and think how I
Shall will them to my children in sweet songs.
Early and late I'm out upon my lands,
And with pleased consequence survey the growth
Of my young trees, acquiring fresh each day,
Although the owners know not that they are
But tenants at my will. I have, in store,
The title-deeds of many a distant wood
And foreign chase. With feeling eye and ear
I have been gifted, and in right of them,
Like a great lord, I walk about the land,
Claiming and dispossessing at my will,—
The belted Earl of many Ennerdales!

REV. F. W. FABER 1814–1863

LARCH TREES

Cumberland

All men speak ill of thee, unlucky Tree!
   Spoiling with graceless line the mountain edge,
   Clothing with awkward sameness rifted ledge,
Or uplands swelling brokenly and free:
Yet shalt thou win some few good words of me.
   Thy boughs it is that teach the wind to mourn,
   Haunting deep inland spots and groves forlorn
With the true murmurs of the plaintive sea.
When tuft and shoot on vernal woodlands shine,
Who hath a green unwinterlike as thine?
And when thou leanest o'er some beetling brow,
   With pale thin twigs the eye can wander through,
There is no other tree on earth but thou
   Which brings the sky so near or makes it seem so blue

from

SIR LANCELOT

The fishy pool
With willow-herb was edged, and with a fringe
Of pithy rush, and tall osmunda's plumes,
And juicy stalks of brittle orpine made;
And a dead hawthorne stood upon the bank,
Whose mossy branches summer yearly clothed
In pointed ruffles of lank bryony,
Rich in autumnal corals that the winds
Unclasp with difficulty from the boughs.
Upon the middle of the bay there swam
A single water-lily, cradled there
In ceaseless agitation: year by year
That lily came, and ever came alone,
By its green cordage anchored in the pool.
So merrily the lively waters shook
The central deep, and made the rushes nod,
And with brisk bubbles round the lily wheeled,
They suffered not the snaky root to spread
Amid the shifting ooze; so there it stayed
With its one yearly blossom from the deep,
Like the old queen of beauty, rising up,
A solitary planet which diffused
A flickering radiance on the bubbles near
And on the rushy rampart of dark green—
A beautiful and waving orb of light.

from

'A LITTLE WHILE'

Yorkshire

There is a spot, 'mid barren hills,
　　Where winter howls, and driving rain;
But, if the dreary tempest chills,
　　There is a light that warms again.

The house is old, the trees are bare,
　Moonless above bends twilight's dome;
But what on earth is half so dear—
　So longed for—as the hearth of home?

The mute bird sitting on the stone,
　The dank moss dripping from the wall,
The thorn-trees gaunt, the walks o'ergrown,
　I love them—how I love them all! . . .

A little and a lone green lane
　That opened on a common wide;
A distant, dreamy, dim blue chain
　Of mountains circling every side.

A heaven so clear, an earth so calm,
　So sweet, so soft, so hushed an air;
And, deepening still the dream-like charm,
　Wild moor-sheep feeding everywhere.

That was the scene, I knew it well;
　I knew the turfy pathway's sweep,
That, winding o'er each billowy swell,
　Marked out the tracks of wandering sheep.

REV. CHARLES KINGSLEY 1819–1875

from

CHRISTMAS DAY

Devonshire

How will it dawn, the coming Christmas Day?
A northern Christmas, such as painters love,
And kinsfolk, shaking hands but once a year,
And dames who tell old legends by the fire?
Red sun, blue sky, white snow, and pearled ice,
Keen ringing air, which sets the blood on fire,
And makes the old man merry with the young,
Through the short sunshine, through the longer night?

Or southern Christmas, dark and dank with mist,
And heavy with the scent of steaming leaves,
And rosebuds mouldering on the dripping porch;
One twilight, without rise or set of sun,
Till beetles drone along the hollow lane,
And round the leafless hawthorns, flitting bats
Hawk the pale moths of winter? Welcome then
At best, the flying gleam, the flying shower,
The rain-pools glittering on the long white roads,
And shadows sweeping on from down to down
Before the salt Atlantic gale: yet come
In whatsoever garb, or gay, or sad,
Come fair, come foul, 'twill still be Christmas Day.

JEAN INGELOW 1820–1897

from

THE FOUR BRIDGES

Lincolnshire

But those old bridges claim another look.
  Our brattling river tumbles through the one;
The second spans a shallow, weedy brook;
  Beneath the others, and beneath the sun,
Lie two long stilly pools, and on their breasts
Picture their wooden piles, encased in swallows' nests.

And round about them grows a fringe of reeds,
  And then a floating crown of lily flowers,
And yet within small silver-budded weeds;
  But each clear centre evermore embowers
A deeper sky, where, stooping, you may see
The little minnows darting restlessly. . . .

[And] the green rushes—O, so glossy green—
  The rushes, they would whisper, rustle, shake;
And forth on floating gauze, no jewelled queen
  So rich, the green-eyed dragon-flies would break,
And hover on the flowers—aërial things,
With little rainbows flickering on their wings.

MATTHEW ARNOLD 1822–1888

THE SCHOLAR GIPSY

Oxfordshire

Go, for they call you, Shepherd, from the hill;
  Go, Shepherd, and untie the wattled cotes:
    No longer leave thy wistful flock unfed,
  Nor let thy bawling fellows rack their throats,
    Nor the cropp'd grasses shoot another head.
      But when the fields are still,
  And the tired men and dogs all gone to rest,
    And only the white sheep are sometimes seen
    Cross and recross the strips of moon-blanch'd green;
  Come, Shepherd, and again renew the quest.

Here, where the reaper was at work of late,
  In this high field's dark corner, where he leaves
    His coat, his basket, and his earthen cruise,
  And in the sun all morning binds the sheaves,
    Then here, at noon, comes back his stores to use:
      Here will I sit and wait,
  While to my ear from uplands far away
    The bleating of the folded flocks is borne,
    With distant cries of reapers in the corn—
  All the live murmur of a summer's day.

Screen'd is this nook o'er the high, half-reap'd field,
  And here till sundown, Shepherd, will I be.
    Through the thick corn the scarlet poppies peep,
  And round green roots and yellowing stalks I see
    Pale blue convolvulus in tendrils creep:
      And air-swept lindens yield
  Their scent, and rustle down their perfumed showers
    Of bloom on the bent grass where I am laid,
    And bower me from the August sun with shade;
  And the eye travels down to Oxford's towers:

And near me on the grass lies Glanvil's book—
   Come, let me read the oft-read tale again,
      The story of that Oxford scholar poor,
   Of pregnant parts and quick inventive brain,
      Who, tir'd of knocking at Preferment's door,
         One summer morn forsook
   His friends, and went to learn the Gipsy lore,
      And roam'd the world with that wild brotherhood,
      And came, as most men deem'd, to little good,
   But came to Oxford and his friends no more.

But once, years after, in the country lanes,
   Two scholars whom at college erst he knew,
      Met him, and of his way of life inquir'd.
   Whereat he answer'd, that the Gipsy crew,
      His mates, had arts to rule as they desir'd
         The workings of men's brains;
   And they can bind them to what thoughts they will:
      'And I,' he said, 'the secret of their art,
      When fully learn'd, will to the world impart:
   But it needs heaven-sent moments for this skill!'

This said, he left them, and return'd no more,
   But rumours hung about the country-side,
      That the lost Scholar long was seen to stray,
   Seen by rare glimpses, pensive and tongue-tied,
      In hat of antique shape, and cloak of grey,
         The same the Gipsies wore.
   Shepherds had met him on the Hurst in spring;
      At some lone alehouse in the Berkshire moors,
      On the warm ingle-bench, the smock-frock'd boors
   Had found him seated at their entering,

But, 'mid their drink and clatter, he would fly:
   And I myself seem half to know thy looks,
      And put the shepherds, Wanderer, on thy trace;
   And boys who in lone wheatfields scare the rooks
      I ask if thou hast pass'd their quiet place;

Stonesfield

Oxfordshire

Or in my boat I lie
Moor'd to the cool bank in the summer heats,
    Mid wide grass meadows which the sunshine fills,
    And watch the warm green-muffled Cumnor hills,
And wonder if thou haunt'st their shy retreats.

For most, I know, thou lov'st retirèd ground.
    Thee, at the ferry, Oxford riders blithe,
        Returning home on summer nights, have met
    Crossing the stripling Thames at Bablock-hithe,
        Trailing in the cool stream thy fingers wet,
            As the slow punt swings round:
        And leaning backwards in a pensive dream,
            And fostering in thy lap a heap of flowers
            Pluck'd in shy fields and distant Wychwood bowers,
        And thine eyes resting on the moonlit stream:

And then they land, and thou art seen no more.
    Maidens who from the distant hamlets come
        To dance around the Fyfield elm in May,
    Oft through the darkening fields have seen thee roam,
        Or cross a stile into the public way.
            Oft thou hast given them store
        Of flowers—the frail-leaf'd, white anemone—
            Dark bluebells drench'd with dews of summer eves—
            And purple orchises with spotted leaves—
        But none has words she can report of thee.

And, above Godstow Bridge, when hay-time's here
    In June, and many a scythe in sunshine flames,
        Men who through those wide fields of breezy grass
    Where black-wing'd swallows haunt the glittering Thames,
        To bathe in the abandon'd lasher pass,
            Have often pass'd thee near
        Sitting upon the river bank o'ergrown:
            Mark'd thy outlandish garb, thy figure spare,
            Thy dark vague eyes, and soft abstracted air;
        But, when they came from bathing, thou wert gone.

At some lone homestead in the Cumnor hills,
  Where at her open door the housewife darns,
    Thou hast been seen, or hanging on a gate
  To watch the threshers in the mossy barns.
    Children, who early range these slopes and late
      For cresses from the rills,
  Have known thee watching, all an April day,
    The springing pastures and the feeding kine;
    And mark'd thee, when the stars come out and shine,
  Through the long dewy grass move slow away.

In Autumn, on the skirts of Bagley wood,
  Where most the Gipsies by the turf-edg'd way
    Pitch their smok'd tents, and every bush you see
  With scarlet patches tagg'd and shreds of grey,
    Above the forest ground call'd Thessaly—
      The blackbird picking food
  Sees thee, nor stops his meal, nor fears at all;
    So often has he known thee past him stray
    Rapt, twirling in thy hand a wither'd spray,
  And waiting for the spark from Heaven to fall.

And once, in winter, on the causeway chill
  Where home through flooded fields foot-travellers go,
    Have I not pass'd thee on the wooden bridge
  Wrapt in thy cloak and battling with the snow,
    Thy face towards Hinksey and its wintry ridge?
      And thou hast climb'd the hill
  And gain'd the white brow of the Cumnor range;
    Turn'd once to watch, while thick the snowflakes fall,
    The line of festal light in Christ-Church hall—
  Then sought thy straw in some sequester'd grange.

But what—I dream! Two hundred years are flown
  Since first thy story ran through Oxford halls,
    And the grave Glanvil did the tale inscribe
  That thou wert wander'd from the studious walls
    To learn strange arts, and join a Gipsy tribe:

And thou from earth art gone
Long since, and in some quiet churchyard laid;
    Some country nook, where o'er thy unknown grave
    Tall grasses and white flowering nettles wave—
Under a dark red-fruited yew-tree's shade.

—No, no, thou hast not felt the lapse of hours.
    For what wears out the life of mortal men?
        'Tis that from change to change their being rolls:
    'Tis that repeated shocks, again, again,
        Exhaust the energy of strongest souls,
            And numb the elastic powers.
    Till having us'd our nerves with bliss and teen,
        And tir'd upon a thousand schemes our wit,
        To the just-pausing Genius we remit
Our worn-out life, and are—what we have been.

MATTHEW ARNOLD 1822–1888

THYRSIS

How changed is here each spot man makes or fills!
    In the two Hinkseys nothing keeps the same;
        The village-street its haunted mansion lacks,
    And from the sign is gone Sibylla's name,
        And from the roofs the twisted chimney-stacks;
            Are ye too changed, ye hills?
    See, 'tis no foot of unfamiliar men
        To-night from Oxford up your pathway strays!
        Here came I often, often, in old days;
Thyrsis and I; we still had Thyrsis then.

Runs it not here, the track by Childsworth Farm,
    Up past the wood, to where the elm-tree crowns
        The hill behind whose ridge the sunset flames?
    The signal-elm, that looks on Ilsley Downs,
        The Vale, the three lone weirs, the youthful Thames?
            This winter-eve is warm,
    Humid the air; leafless, yet soft as spring,
        The tender purple spray on copse and briers;
        And that sweet City with her dreaming spires,
She needs not June for beauty's heightening.

Lovely all times she lies, lovely to-night!
Only, methinks, some loss of habit's power
Befalls me wandering through this upland dim;
Once pass'd I blindfold here, at any hour;
Now seldom come I, since I came with him.
That single elm-tree bright
Against the west—I miss it! is it gone?
We prized it dearly; while it stood, we said,
Our friend, the Scholar-Gipsy, was not dead;
While the tree lived, he in these fields lived on.

Too rare, too rare, grow now my visits here!
But once I knew each field, each flower, each stick;
And with the country-folk acquaintance made
By barn in threshing-time, by new-built rick.
Here, too, our shepherd-pipes we first essay'd.
Ah me! this many a year
My pipe is lost, my shepherd's-holiday!
Needs must I lose them, needs with heavy heart
Into the world and wave of men depart;
But Thyrsis of his own will went away.

It irk'd him to be here, he could not rest.
He loved each simple joy the country yields,
He loved his mates; but yet he could not keep,
For that a shadow lour'd on the fields,
Here with the shepherds and the silly sheep.
Some life of men unblest
He knew, which made him droop, and fill'd his head.
He went; his piping took a troubled sound
Of storms that rage outside our happy ground;
He could not wait their passing, he is dead!

So, some tempestuous morn in early June,
When the year's primal burst of bloom is o'er,
Before the roses and the longest day—
When garden-walks, and all the grassy floor,
With blossoms, red and white, of fallen May,

And chestnut-flowers are strewn—
So have I heard the cuckoo's parting cry,
    From the wet field, through the vext garden-trees,
    Come with the volleying rain and tossing breeze:
The bloom is gone, and with the bloom go I.

Too quick despairer, wherefore wilt thou go?
    Soon will the high Midsummer pomps come on,
        Soon will the musk carnations break and swell,
    Soon shall we have gold-dusted snapdragon,
        Sweet-William with its homely cottage-smell,
            And stocks in fragrant blow;
    Roses that down the alleys shine afar,
        And open, jasmine-muffled lattices,
        And groups under the dreaming garden-trees,
    And the full moon, and the white evening-star.

He hearkens not! light comer, he is flown!
    What matters it? next year he will return,
        And we shall have him in the sweet spring-days,
    With whitening hedges, and uncrumpling fern,
        And blue-bells trembling by the forest-ways,
            And scent of hay new-mown.
    But Thyrsis never more we swains shall see!
        See him come back, and cut a smoother reed,
        And blow a strain the world at last shall heed—
    For Time, not Corydon, hath conquer'd thee.

Alack, for Corydon no rival now!—
    But when Sicilian shepherds lost a mate,
        Some good survivor with his flute would go,
    Piping a ditty sad for Bion's fate,
        And cross the unpermitted ferry's flow,
            And relax Pluto's brow,
    And make leap up with joy the beauteous head
        Of Proserpine, among whose crownèd hair
        Are flowers, first open'd on Sicilian air,
    And flute his friend, like Orpheus, from the dead.

O easy access to the hearer's grace
  When Dorian shepherds sang to Proserpine!
    For she herself had trod Sicilian fields,
  She knew the Dorian water's gush divine,
    She knew each lily white which Enna yields,
      Each rose with blushing face;
  She loved the Dorian pipe, the Dorian strain,
    But ah, of our poor Thames she never heard!
    Her foot the Cumnor cowslips never stirr'd!
And we should tease her with our plaint in vain.

Well! wind-dispers'd and vain the words will be,
  Yet, Thyrsis, let me give my grief its hour
    In the old haunt, and find our tree-topp'd hill!
  Who, if not I, for questing here hath power?
    I know the wood which hides the daffodil,
      I know the Fyfield tree,
  I know what white, what purple fritillaries
    The grassy harvest of the river-fields,
    Above by Eynsham, down by Sandford, yields,
And what sedg'd brooks are Thames's tributaries;

I know these slopes; who knows them if not I?
  But many a dingle on the loved hill-side,
    With thorns once studded, old, white-blossom'd trees,
  Where thick the cowslips grew, and, far descried,
    High tower'd the spikes of purple orchises,
      Hath since our day put by
  The coronals of that forgotten time.
    Down each green bank hath gone the ploughboy's team,
    And only in the hidden brookside gleam
Primroses, orphans of the flowery prime.

Where is the girl, who, by the boatman's door,
  Above the locks, above the boating throng,
    Unmoor'd our skiff, when, through the Wytham flats,
  Red loosestrife and blond meadow-sweet among,
    And darting swallows, and light water-gnats,

We track'd the shy Thames shore?
Where are the mowers, who, as the tiny swell
Of our boat passing heav'd the river-grass,
Stood with suspended scythe to see us pass?
They all are gone, and thou art gone as well.

Yes, thou are gone! and round me too the night
In ever-nearing circle weaves her shade.
I see her veil draw soft across the day,
I feel her slowly chilling breath invade
The cheek grown thin, the brown hair sprent with grey;
I feel her finger light
Laid pausefully upon life's headlong train;
The foot less prompt to meet the morning dew,
The heart less bounding at emotion new,
And hope, once crush'd, less quick to spring again.

And long the way appears, which seem'd so short
To the unpractis'd eye of sanguine youth;
And high the mountain-tops, in cloudy air,
The mountain-tops where is the throne of Truth,
Tops in life's morning-sun so bright and bare!
Unbreachable the fort
Of the long-batter'd world uplifts its wall.
And strange and vain the earthly turmoil grows,
And near and real the charm of thy repose,
And night as welcome as a friend would fall.

But hush! the upland hath a sudden loss
Of quiet;—Look! adown the dusk hill-side,
A troop of Oxford hunters going home,
As in old days, jovial and talking, ride!
From hunting with the Berkshire hounds they come–
Quick, let me fly, and cross
Into yon further field!—'Tis done; and see,
Back'd by the sunset, which doth glorify
The orange and pale violet evening-sky,
Bare on its lonely ridge, the Tree! the Tree!

I take the omen! Eve lets down her veil,
　　The white fog creeps from bush to bush about,
　　　The west unflushes, the high stars grow bright,
　　And in the scatter'd farms the lights come out.
　　　I cannot reach the Signal-Tree to-night,
　　　　Yet, happy omen, hail!
　　Hear it from thy broad lucent Arno-vale
　　　(For there thine earth-forgetting eyelids keep
　　　The morningless and unawakening sleep
　　Under the flowery oleanders pale),

Hear it, O Thyrsis, still our Tree is there!—
　　Ah vain! These English fields, this upland dim,
　　　These brambles pale with mist engarlanded,
　　That lone, sky-pointing tree, are not for him.
　　　To a boon southern country he is fled,
　　　　And now in happier air,
　　Wandering with the great Mother's train divine
　　　(And purer or more subtle soul than thee,
　　　I trow, the mighty Mother doth not see!)
　　Within a folding of the Apennine,

Thou hearest the immortal strains of old.
　　Putting his sickle to the perilous grain
　　　In the hot cornfield of the Phrygian king,
　　For thee the Lityerses song again
　　　Young Daphnis with his silver voice doth sing;
　　　　Sings his Sicilian fold,
　　His sheep, his hapless love, his blinded eyes;
　　　And how a call celestial round him rang
　　　And heavenward from the fountain-brink he sprang,
　　And all the marvel of the golden skies.

There thou art gone, and me thou leavest here
　　Sole in these fields; yet will I not despair;
　　　Despair I will not, while I yet descry
　　'Neath the soft canopy of English air
　　　That lonely Tree against the western sky.

Still, still these slopes, 'tis clear,
Our Gipsy-Scholar haunts, outliving thee!
    Fields where soft sheep from cages pull the hay,
    Woods with anemones in flower till May,
Know him a wanderer still; then why not me?

A fugitive and gracious light he seeks,
    Shy to illumine; and I seek it too.
        This does not come with houses or with gold,
    With place, with honour, and a flattering crew;
        'Tis not in the world's market bought and sold.
        But the smooth-slipping weeks
    Drop by, and leave its seeker still untired;
        Out of the heed of mortals he is gone,
        He wends unfollow'd, he must house alone;
    Yet on he fares, by his own heart inspired.

Thou too, O Thyrsis, on like quest wert bound,
    Thou wanderedst with me for a little hour;
        Men gave thee nothing, but this happy quest,
    If men esteem'd thee feeble, gave thee power,
        If men procured thee trouble, gave thee rest.
        And this rude Cumnor ground,
    Its fir-topped Hurst, its farms, its quiet fields,
        Here cam'st thou in thy jocund youthful time,
        Here was thine height of strength, thy golden prime;
    And still the haunt beloved a virtue yields.

What though the music of thy rustic flute
    Kept not for long its happy, country tone,
        Lost it too soon, and learnt a stormy note
    Of men contention-tost, of men who groan,
        Which task'd thy pipe too sore, and tired thy throat—
            It fail'd, and thou wast mute;
    Yet hadst thou alway visions of our light,
        And long with men of care thou couldst not stay,
        And soon thy foot resumed its wandering way,
    Left human haunt, and on alone till night.

Too rare, too rare, grow now my visits here!
'Mid city-noise, not, as with thee of yore,
Thyrsis, in reach of sheep-bells is my home!
Then through the great town's harsh, heart-wearying roar
Let in thy voice a whisper often come,
To chase fatigue and fear:
Why faintest thou? I wander'd till I died.
Roam on! the light we sought is shining still.
Dost thou ask proof? Our Tree yet crowns the hill,
Our Scholar travels yet the loved hillside.

COVENTRY PATMORE 1823–1896

from –

THE ANGEL IN THE HOUSE

Wiltshire

Once more I came to Sarum Close,
With joy half memory, half desire,
And breathed the sunny wind that rose
And blew the shadows o'er the Spire,
And toss'd the lilac's scented plumes,
And sway'd the chestnut's thousand cones,
And fill'd my nostrils with perfumes,
And shaped the clouds in waifs and zones,
And wafted down the serious strain
Of Sarum bells, when, true to time,
I reach'd the Dean's, with heart and brain
That trembled to the trembling chime.

'Twas half my home, six years ago.
The six years had not alter'd it:
Red-brick and ashlar, long and low,
With dormers and with oriels lit.
Geranium, lychnis, rose array'd
The windows, all wide open thrown;
And some one in the Study play'd
The Wedding-March of Mendelssohn.

from

TAMERTON CHURCH TOWER

Devonshire

The gaps of blue shrank fast in span;
  The long-forgotten breeze,
By lazy starts and fits, began
  To stir the higher trees.
At noon, we came to Tavistock;
  And sunshine still was there,
But gloomy Dartmoor seem'd to mock
  Its weak and yellow glare.
The swallows in the wrathful light
  Were pitching up and down;
A string of rooks made rapid flight,
  Due southward, o'er the town,
Where, baiting at the Tiger-Inn,
  We talk'd by windows wide,
Of Blanche and all my unseen kin,
  Who did our coming bide.

The heavy sign-board swung and shriek'd,
  In dark air whirl'd the vane,
Blinds flapp'd, dust rose, and, straining, creak'd
  The shaken window-pane;
And, just o'erhead, a huge cloud flung,
  For earnest of its stores,
A few calm drops, that struck among
  The light-leaved sycamores . . .
The string of rooks had travell'd on,
  Against the southern shroud,
And, like some snaky skeleton,
  Lay twisted in the cloud.

from

THE RIVER

It is a venerable place,
　An old ancestral ground,
So broad, the rainbow wholly stands
　Within its lordly bound;
And there the river waits and winds
　By many a wooded mound.

Upon a rise, where single oaks
　And clumps of beeches tall
Drop pleasantly their shade beneath,
　Half-hid amidst them all,
Stands in its quiet dignity
　An ancient manor-hall.

About its many gable-ends
　The swallows wheel their flight;
The huge fantastic weather-vanes
　Look happy in the light;
The warm front through the foliage gleams,
　A comfortable sight.

The ivied turrets seem to love
　The low, protected leas;
And, though this manor-hall hath seen
　The snow of centuries,
How freshly still it stands amid
　Its wealth of swelling trees!

The leafy summer-time is young;
　The yearling lambs are strong;
The sunlight glances merrily;
　The trees are full of song;
The valley-loving river flows
　Contentedly along.

SONNET

I walk of grey noons by the old canal
   Where rain-drops patter on the autumn leaves,
Now watching from some ivied orchard wall
   In slopes of stubble figures pile the sheaves;
Or under banks in shadow of their grass,
   Blue water-flies by starts jettingly pass
'Mid large leaves level on the glassy cool;
   Or noiseless dizzy midges winking round
The yellow sallows of the meadow pool;
   While into cloudy silence ebbs each sound,
And sifts the moulting sunlight warm and mellow
   O'er sandy beach remote, or slumberous flood,
Or rooky red brick mansion by the wood,
   Mossed gate, or farmyard hay-stack tanned and yellow.

WILLIAM ALLINGHAM 1824–1889

from

BY THE WAY

Surrey

                  You see
Nestled into a hollow of the downs,
Where sheep stray widely o'er the short green turf,
A little gray-walled church with lichened roof;
A farmyard and a huge old barn whose stacks
O'er-top the spire; the farmhouse lattices
Embowered with vine; a figtreed garden wall;
And one clump of rook-nested elms above
Gables and red tiled roofs and twisted chimneys.

APETHORPE

Northamptonshire

The moss-grey mansion of my father stands
Park'd in an English pasturage as fair
As any that the grass-green isle can show.
Above it rise deep-wooded lawns; below
A brook runs riot thro' the pleasant lands,
And blabs its secret to the merry air.
The village peeps from out deep poplars, where
A grey bridge spans the stream; and all beyond,
In sloping vales and sweet acclivities,
The many-dimpled, laughing landscapes lies.
Four-square, and double-courted, and grey-stoned,
Two quaint quadrangles of deep-latticed walls,
Grass-grown, and moaned about by troops of doves,
The ancient House! Collegiate in name,
As in its aspect, like the famous Halls
Whose hoary fronts make reverend the groves
Of Isis, or the banks of classic Cam.

LORD DE TABLEY 1835–1895

RURAL EVENING

Cheshire

The whip cracks on the plough-team's flank,
  The thresher's flail beats duller.
The round of day has warmed a bank
  Of cloud to primrose colour.

The dairy girls cry home the kine,
  The kine in answer lowing;
And rough-haired louts with sleepy shouts
  Keep crows whence seed is growing.

The creaking wain, brushed through the lane,
  Hangs straws on hedges narrow;
And smoothly cleaves the soughing plough,
  And harsher grinds the harrow.

Comes, from the road-side inn caught up,
  A brawl of crowded laughter,
Thro' falling brooks and cawing rooks
  A fiddle scrambling after.

DAVID GRAY 1838–1861

from

OCTOBER

Stirling

O, the sweet melancholy of the time
When gently, ere the heart appeals, the year
Shines in the fatal beauty of decay!
When the sun sinks enlarged on Carronben,
Nakedly visible, without a cloud,
And faintly from the faint eternal blue
(That dim, sweet hairbell-colour) comes the star
Which evening wears—when Luggie flows in mist,
And in the cottage windows, one by one,
With sudden twinkle household lamps are lit—
What noiseless falling of the faded leaf!

DAVID GRAY 1838–1861

TO A FRIEND

Dumbarton

Now, while the long delaying ash assumes
  The delicate April green, and, loud and clear,
Through the cool, yellow, mellow twilight-glooms,
  The thrush's song enchants the captive ear;

117

Now, while a shower is pleasant in the falling,
    Stirring the still perfume that wakes around;
Now that doves mourn, and from the distance calling,
    The cuckoo answers with a sovereign sound—
Come with thy native heart, O true and tried!
    But leave all books; for what with converse high,
Flavoured with Attic wit, the time shall glide
    On smoothly, as a river floweth by,
Or, as on stately pinion through the grey
Evening, the culver cuts his liquid way.

DAVID GRAY 1838–1861

THE BROOKLET

O deep unlovely brooklet, moaning slow
    Thro' moorish fen in utter loneliness!
The partridge wavers beside the loamy flow
    In pulseful tremor, when with sudden press
The huntsman flusters thro' the rustled heather.
    In March thy sallow-buds from vermeil shells
Break, satin-tinted, downy as the feather
    Of moss-chat that among the purplish bells
Breasts into fresh new life her three unborn.
    The plover hovers o'er thee, uttering clear
And mournful-strange, his human cry forlorn:
    While wearily, alone, and void of cheer
Thou glid'st thy nameless waters from the fen,
To sleep unsunned in an untrampled glen.

INDEX OF AUTHORS

INDEX OF COUNTIES